Treating Anxiety Disorders

Rodrigo A. Muñoz, *Editor*
University of California, San Diego

NEW DIRECTIONS FOR MENTAL HEALTH SERVICES
H. RICHARD LAMB, *Editor-in-Chief*
University of Southern California

Number 32, Winter 1986

Paperback sourcebooks in
The Jossey-Bass Social and Behavioral Sciences Series

Jossey-Bass Inc., Publishers
San Francisco • London

Rodrigo A. Muñoz (ed.).
Treating Anxiety Disorders.
New Directions for Mental Health Services, no. 32.
San Francisco: Jossey-Bass, 1986.

New Directions for Mental Health Services
H. Richard Lamb, *Editor-in-Chief*

New Directions for Mental Health Services (publication number USPS 493-910) is published quarterly by Jossey-Bass Inc., Publishers. Second class postage paid at San Francisco, California, and at additional mailing offices. POSTMASTER: Send address changes to Jossey-Bass Inc., Publishers, 433 California Street, San Francisco, California 94104.

Editorial correspondence should be sent to the Editor-in-Chief, H. Richard Lamb, Department of Psychiatry and the Behavioral Sciences, U.S.C. School of Medicine, 1934 Hospital Place, Los Angeles, California 90033.

Library of Congress Catalog Card Number 85-81896

International Standard Serial Number ISSN 0193-9416

International Standard Book Number ISBN 1-55542-989-0

Cover art by WILLI BAUM

Manufactured in the United States of America

Ordering Information

The paperback sourcebooks listed below are published quarterly and can be ordered either by subscription or single-copy.

Subscriptions cost $40.00 per year for institutions, agencies, and libraries. Individuals can subscribe at the special rate of $30.00 per year *if payment is by personal check.* (Note that the full rate of $40.00 applies if payment is by institutional check, even if the subscription is designated for an individual.) Standing orders are accepted.

Single copies are available at $9.95 when payment accompanies order, and *all single-copy orders under $25.00 must include payment.* (California, New Jersey, New York, and Washington, D.C., residents please include appropriate sales tax.) For billed orders, cost per copy is $9.95 plus postage and handling. (Prices subject to change without notice.)

Bulk orders (ten or more copies) of any individual sourcebook are available at the following discounted prices: 10–49 copies, $8.95 each; 50–100 copies, $7.96 each; over 100 copies, *inquire.* Sales tax and postage and handling charges apply as for single copy orders.

Please note that these prices are for the academic year 1986–1987 and are subject to change without prior notice. Also, some titles may be out of print and therefore not available for sale.

To ensure correct and prompt delivery, all orders must give either the *name of an individual* or an *official purchase order number.* Please submit your order as follows:

Subscriptions: specify series and year subscription is to begin.
Single Copies: specify sourcebook code (such as, MHS1) and first two words of title.

Mail orders for United States and Possessions, Latin America, Canada, Japan, Australia, and New Zealand to:
Jossey-Bass Inc., Publishers
433 California Street
San Francisco, California 94104

Mail orders for all other parts of the world to:
Jossey-Bass Limited
28 Banner Street
London EC1Y 8QE

New Directions for Mental Health Services Series
H. Richard Lamb, *Editor-in-Chief*

MHS1 *Alternatives to Acute Hospitalization,* H. Richard Lamb
MHS2 *Community Support Systems for the Long-Term Patient,* Leonard I. Stein
MHS3 *Mental Health Consultations in Community Settings,* Alexander S. Rogawski

MHS4 *Coping With the Legal Onslaught,* Seymour L. Halleck
MHS5 *Adolescence: Perspectives on Psychotherapy,* Sherman C. Feinstein
MHS6 *Crisis Intervention in the 1980s,* Gerald F. Jackobson
MHS7 *The Fairweather Lodge: A Twenty-Five Year Retrospective,* George W. Fairweather
MHS8 *Middle Management in Mental Health,* Stephen L. White
MHS9 *Perspectives on Rural Mental Health,* Morton O. Wagenfeld
MHS10 *The Alcoholism Services Delivery System,* Alfonso Paredes
MHS11 *Issues in Community Residential Care,* Richard D. Budson
MHS12 *New Developments in Interventions with Families of Schizophrenics,* Michael J. Goldstein
MHS13 *Mental Health Promotion and Primary Prevention,* Felice Davidson Perlmutter
MHS14 *The Young Adult Chronic Patient,* Bert Pepper, Hilary Ryglewicz
MHS15 *Treatment for Psychosomatic Problems,* John M. Kuldau
MHS16 *The Mental Health Professional and the Legal System,* Bruce H. Gross, Linda E. Weinberger
MHS17 *Deinstitutionalization,* Leona L. Bachrach
MHS18 *Unified Mental Health Systems: Utopia Unrealized,* John A. Talbott
MHS19 *Effective Aftercare for the 1980s,* David L. Cutler
MHS20 *Advances in Occupational Mental Health,* Stephen L. White
MHS21 *Advances in Treating the Young Adult Chronic Patient,* Bert Pepper, Hilary Ryglewicz
MHS22 *Patterns of Adolescent Self-Image,* Daniel Offer, Eric Ostrov, Kenneth I. Howard
MHS23 *Therapeutic Potential of Mood Disorders Clinics,* Rodrigo A. Muñoz
MHS24 *Intervention Among Psychiatrically Disabled Parents and Their Young Children,* Bertram J. Cohler, Judith S. Musick
MHS25 *Legal Encroachment on Psychiatric Practice,* Stephen Rachlin
MHS26 *The Training in Community Living Model: A Decade of Experience,* Leonard I. Stein, Mary Ann Test
MHS27 *Clinical Issues in Treating the Chronic Mentally Ill,* Joel S. Kanter
MHS28 *Emergency Psychiatry at the Crossroads,* Frank Lipton, Stephen M. Goldfinger
MHS29 *The Elderly and Chronic Mental Illness,* Nancy S. Abramson, Jean K. Quam, Mona Wasow
MHS30 *The Mental Health Needs of Homeless Persons,* Ellen L. Bassuk
MHS31 *Eating Disorders,* Felix E. F. Larocca

Contents

Editor's Notes

The field of anxiety disorders is changing rapidly. As we were writing this volume, new information kept demanding changes in the concepts we were discussing. A new nomenclature for anxiety disorders was proposed to the Board of Trustees of the American Psychiatric Association at the time we were trying to present a scheme for differential diagnosis in Chapter Three. On occasion we cited papers not yet published. The atmosphere of change and clarification influenced our choice of subjects and the specific items we thought most relevant to clinical practice today.

Chapter One presents an overview of anxiety disorders, with examples of generalized anxiety disorder, panic discorder, phobic disorder, obsessive-compulsive disorder, and post-traumatic stress disorder. It closes with a statement on resiliency and anxiety. Both vulnerability and resistance to a disorder could obey to inherited or environmental factors. The clinician may look beyond a rigid adherence to a theory to deal with specific factors attending each case.

Anxiety disorders are ubiquitous. As pointed out in Chapter Two, fears and anxieties are part of the normal pattern of development and the normal pattern of living. In order to study pathological fears, a clear conception has to be obtained about their incidence and prevalence. Dr. Reich makes a major effort to provide the necessary information.

Chapter Three was perhaps the most demanding in the book. We had a number of meeting with the authors, discussing old and new information and formulating our best ideas as to what may be considered true in the late 1980s and the 1990s. The nomenclature will likely revert to a basic picture of panic disorder that may be associated with limited phobias, social phobias, and agoraphobia. The differential diagnosis from affective disorders and from "organic anxiety" will continue to bedevil the classifiers.

As in the field of mood disorders, the debate about the relative value of verbal and somatic therapies in anxiety disorders will continue for the foreseeable future. While cognitive therapy has been presented persuasively as a treatment of choice, many hail the advent of the new antianxiety compounds as a very promising alternative. In Chapter Four Dr. Bowers develops a solid case for the use of cognitive therapy and gives precise instructions about its use.

Every effort has been made to present the case for the study and treatment of anxiety disorders in childhood. Chapter Five indicates that anxiety produces a significant amount of pain and dysfunction among children. It evaluates the meaning of anxiety in childhood, the possible factors leading to the development and control of anxiety, and the areas that require more research.

If the other chapters have convinced the reader that he or she should develop a program for anxiety disorders, we want to offer guidance on how to do it. Sue Erskine has been very successful in developing a comprehensive program for the treatment of anxiety disorders in San Diego, California. Chapter Six is a distillate of the thinking that went into the anxiety disorders clinic developed at Harbor View Medical Center in San Diego by the Western Mood and Sleep Disorders Institute. I have tried to summarize in Chapter Seven what is currently accepted in relation to somatic therapies for anxiety, as well as to give an overview of the most pressing problems that are currently debated in the psychiatric literature.

Rodrigo A. Muñoz
Editor

Rodrigo A. Muñoz is associate professor of clinical psychiatry at the University of California at San Diego, president of the American Academy of Clinical Psychiatrists, and president of the Western Mood and Sleep Disorders Institute in San Diego.

Five types of anxiety disorders are recognized. They are presented and discussed in this chapter.

Anxiety Disorders

Rodrigo A. Muñoz

Anxiety disorders are receiving much attention in psychiatric practice today because they are common, they are disabling, and they are treatable. This chapter and the following answer a number of questions.

Are anxiety disorders the same as panic attacks? As this chapter and the second will explain, disorders related to anxiety include panic attacks but also several other disorders. Panic attacks have become the best known and the best studied. This is the reason for devoting a chapter to them.

Are there tests for panic disorders? Chapter Two reviews this question. Those now researched are certainly at the frontier of much progress that will permit scientific accuracy in our diagnosis and treatments.

Are there any organic disorders related to panic attacks? The differential diagnosis of anxiety disorders is becoming one of the critical areas of study. This book will present what has developed in recent years.

What is the most effective treatment? The jury is still out. While the majority of treated patients have required medications, verbal therapies are increasingly effective in selected groups of patients.

For this initial chapter, out of the wealth of information recently available, we want to center on the writing of two experts: Donald Goodwin, M.D. and Michael Rutter, M.D., F.R.C.P. Dr. Goodwin (1986) defines anxiety as an emotion that signifies the presence of a danger that either cannot be identified or, if identified, is not sufficiently threatening to justify the intensity of the emotion.

R. A. Muñoz (ed.). *Treating Anxiety Disorders.*
New Directions for Mental Health Services, no. 32. San Francisco: Jossey-Bass, Winter 1986.

Generalized Anxiety Disorder

This is a condition that "usually begins in late adolescence or early adulthood, and is manifested by persistent feelings of tension, jitteriness, being on edge—as if something terrible may happen in any minute" (Goodwin, 1986).

We do not see many patients with this disorder in general psychiatric practice. Probably they go to other professionals and only come to us when suffering psychiatric disorders that usually started after the anxiety problems.

Case A. Dr. A is sixty-two years old. He has never had formal psychiatric treatment. We would not have become aware of his disorder had we not worked closely with him for many years, during which time he has discussed his symptoms and his distresses with us almost on a regular basis. He has answered any suggestion that he should undergo psychotherapy or receive medication with a long speech on anxiety as a major source of productivity.

We never saw Dr. A sit down and enjoy anything. When he is not moving his legs, he is drumming on the table with his fingers, looking at other people, and getting concerned because something is too early, too late, too fast, too slow, too important, too difficult, or too something else. Somebody said Dr. A "perspires anxiety." Most co-workers find it impossible to relax around Dr. A.

For some of those who know Dr. A better, he behaves as if there is an invisible barrier between him and many activities that he never undertook because of possible stress or danger. He had been a swimmer in high school, but he never swam again after he graduated, for fear that he might have a medical problem while in the water and drown. He would not venture into the woods ("there may be a wild hunter seeking a victim") or in the snow ("you may break a leg without any need"); a baseball fan, he always sits as high as possible at the stadium to avoid being hit by stray balls. He keeps careful records of his wife's and children's health history.

Dr. A is known for his conservative approach to his patient's care. He often uses consultants and at times appears to be more a broker of medical care than a treating physician. He explains the situation by insisting that he is providing the very best to the very few patients he can see.

Research published recently has shown that many patients with generalized anxiety disorder also suffer panic attacks and probably could be better classified as suffering a panic disorder. The small group without panic disorders is the only one that should be classified as suffering generalized anxiety disorder.

Panic Disorder

The initial characteristic of this disorder is panic attacks, described as discrete period of apprehension or fear accompanied by somatic symptoms including dyspnea, palpitations, chest pain or discomfort, choking, dizziness, cold and hot flashes, sweating, fainting, and trembling. Panic disorders are probably the most typical and best studied of the anxiety disorders.

Case B. By any possible standards, Ms. B was a very courageous police officer. She participated in dangerous work, often as a volunteer and in situations of immediate danger to her life. She had been wounded and commended frequently and was often described as a fearless person.

Ms. B consulted our clinic after much encouragement by her supervisors. She had visited several cardiologists, had undergone a number of evaluations, and was still convinced that she suffered an organic disorder affecting her heart. She did not consider herself a nervous person, but in the last three years—she was now twenty-seven years old—she had had as many as seven discrete episodes of sudden distress, apprehension, and feelings of impending doom, accompanied by palpitations, chest pain, shortness of breath, and a choking sensation. She had identified her symptoms as those typical for "a heart attack," had adhered even more closely to a stringent diet, and had enhanced an exhausting exercise routine in order to correct the situation. Reassurance by the cardiologists that all studies were normal had failed to produce any change in Ms. B's belief and attitude.

Phobic Disorders

A phobia is a persistent, excessive, unreasonable fear of a specific object, activity, or situation that results in a compelling desire to avoid the dreaded object, activity, or situation.

The phobic disorders are divided into three types: agoraphobia, the most common and severe form; social phobia; and simple phobia.

1. In agoraphobia "the individual has marked fear of, and thus avoids, being alone or in public places from which escape might be difficult, or when help is not available in case of sudden incapacitation, such as in crowds, tunnels, bridges, public transportation" (APA, 1980).

2. A social phobia is "a persistent, irrational fear of, a compelling desire to avoid, a situation in which the individual is exposed to possible scrutiny by others, and fears that he or she may act in a way that will be humiliating or embarrassing" (APA, 1980).

3. A simple phobia is "a persistent, irrational fear of, and compelling desire to avoid, an object or situation other than being alone, or in public places away from home (agoraphobia), or of humiliation or embarrassment in social situations (social phobia)" (APA, 1980).

Phobias are likely the most common mental health problems in the U.S. Among psychiatric patients being treated for other disorders, more than half may suffer phobias. In patients being treated for fractures, prevalence of agoraphobia and social phobias may be as high as 30 percent.

Case C. Ms. C had many talents and many fears. She came from a very religious family that held rigid standards. Ms. C remembered when her maternal aunt, the sister of a priest, pronounced her suitable for a convent. Ms. C shared the positive family response because this meant minimal contact with other human beings. She wanted to devote herself exclusively to religious pursuits, but she was sent to an order that put her through college and helped her obtain a degree in education. She was a very shy person who suffered great apprehension every time she had to talk in class. She went through school always feeling apprehensive, worried, and tense, especially in the presence of others. After graduation, her classroom experience was a complete failure. She could express her ideas clearly and convincingly, but she could not keep the children's attention; she usually ended up in a state of consternation and anguish. She eventually left her order to become a private tutor.

The happiest years of her life were those she spent helping in the education of a wealthy boy who had suffered extensive perinatal brain damage and was blind and deaf. This job terminated when the child had grown old enough to attend a special school; Ms. C then had a very difficult time obtaining employment that was suitable to her fears. After much help from friends, she found a sales job that she thought was appropriate. She went to work at a large shoe store, mostly helping the customers try on new shoes. She was happy as long as she obtained help from other sales people so that she did not have to interact much with the customers. When she was eventually promoted to assistant manager, her anxiety and apprehension became constant and she had to resign. After several months of unemployment, she became an assistant draftsperson at a large technology firm, where she was very successful as long as she was left alone working on a specific project.

When we met Ms. C, she was a forty-two-year-old single woman who was still drafting in almost total social isolation. She described multiple fears of people, places, and specific situations, especially those related to talking to groups. She described her life as having become that of a hermit so that she could avoid the situations that produced anxiety. She sounded as if she could live for periods of weeks or months not suffering much apprehension as long as her life was regulated by very rigid avoidance of many situations.

Obsessive-Compulsive Disorders

The essential features of obsessive-compulsive disorders are recurrent obsessions or compulsions.

Obsessions are recurrent and persistent ideas, thoughts, images, or impulses that are ego-dystonic. They are not experienced as voluntarily produced but rather as though they invade consciousness and are experienced as senseless or repugnant. Attempts are made to ignore or suppress them.

Compulsions are repetitive and seemingly purposeful behaviors that are performed according to certain rules or in a stereotyped fashion. The behavior is not an end in itself but is designed to produce or prevent some future event or situation. The activity either is not connected in a realistic way with what it is designed to produce or prevent, or is clearly excessive. The act is performed with a sense of subjective compulsion coupled with a desire to resist the compulsion (at least initially). The individual generally recognizes the senselessness of the behavior (this may not be true for young children) and does not derive pleasure from carrying out the activity, although it provides a release of tension. Obsessive-compulsive disorders are said to occur in 1 percent or less of the adult population, but they are quite severe in many cases and often interfere greatly with the person's functioning.

Case D. We have known for a number of years this forty-eight-year-old woman whose life centered on four different themes.

Insects and insecticides. Ever since she was a child, the patient has had recurrent thoughts that insects will control all human beings and humanity will be exterminated in the process of using insecticides. She has spent days on end checking her house to make sure there are no ants, spraying insecticide to make sure the ants will not come, and then washing and cleaning everything in sight to make sure that no one gets accidentally poisoned with the insecticide. The rituals have become accepted by her husband and children, who even help, sometimes daily, in the inspection for ants, the fumigation, and the cleaning of insecticide. The patient is an authority on the longevity of most insecticides but often calls the Poison Control Center to inquire whether any of her children could possibly have been poisoned, either when they were spraying or when they were eating at home after the insecticide had been removed with soap and water.

Insurance coverage. The patient is very well known to the company that insures her husband's employer. She spends endless hours reading insurance policies and any other information about the coverage she is entitled to. She checks and rechecks the payments the insurance company has made on any medical care for her family, for excessive payments or for conditions not covered. When her son developed prognathism, a deformity of the jaw, the company was willing to pay for a reduction of the jaw, but the woman was reluctant to accept the offer, saying that the jaw "had grown on its own," which meant that prognathism was a "congenital condition," not covered by the insurance. On one occasion the patient called the company about coverage that had occurred ten years before, the documents for which were no longer available. Reassurance by the company that no one would take action against her on such an old claim failed to stop the patient's ruminations about possible fraud.

Sin. The patient is a devout Catholic. She has gone through periods during which she confessed the same sins daily for several weeks. At the request of her therapist, a pastoral counselor advised her that because she was "mentally ill" she could not commit any more sins and therefore was free to receive communion as often as she wanted to. This produced a short period of relief until the patient developed doubts about the authority of the counselor and started trying to document his training and the authority he had to advise her.

Marriage and divorce. The patient has been married for twenty-five years but has never been able to make up her mind whether she loves her husband and should stay married to him or should divorce him. She has filled a number of notebooks with daily notes about the pros and cons of divorce. About ten years ago, after three children, she decided not to have sex with her husband anymore on account that should she ever divorce him, it would have been a sin to have sex with him. The husband, an ever-accepting and supporting person, has generally gone along with the patient and has adapted to her numerous decisions and rules.

Post-Traumatic Stress Disorder

This is the most controversial of the pictures associated with anxiety. The criteria include:

1. existence of a recognizable stressor that would evoke significant symptoms of distress in almost everyone;
2. re-experiencing of the trauma; numbing of responsiveness to or reduced involvement with the external world; and
3. symptoms that suggest a reaction to trauma, such as hyperalertness, sleep disturbance, guilt about surviving, memory impairment, avoidance of activities that arouse recollection of the traumatic event, or intensification of symptoms by exposure to events that symbolize or resemble the traumatic event.

According to Goodwin, the disorder seems to wax and wane according to the frequency of massive tragedies of war. During the American Civil War, the disorder was called "nostalgia" and initially treated with hospitalization. When the policy changed and the victims were jailed, the incidence fell to zero. General Patton, "believed war neurosis should be punishable by death, an approach pioneered by the Russians with outstanding success" (Goodwin, 1986). We expect the debate about the existence and meaning of post-traumatic disorders to continue for the forseeable future.

Case E. Ms. E came from a small town in Romania. She and her husband migrated to the United States when she was thirty-five years old. He was a nuclear physicist and soon found work in a high technology concern. She was a chemist who also became employed shortly after arriving in California. Eighteen months after initiating her new life, she was involved in a car accident in which, while her husband was driving, their car was hit by a drunk driver. The car was thrown off the highway and against a tree. Ms. E and her husband both suffered a number of bruises but no serious injury. Both were discharged from the emergency room after they had been evaluated.

We saw Ms. E at the request of the attorney for her insurance company. She was not familiar with legal procedures, insurance companies, or the litigation that often follows automobile accidents in America. She was satisfied to be alive and pleased that she might be able to get another car. The rest was of less importance to her.

During our first interview, Ms. E reported recurrent nightmares about the accident. She also complained about panic attacks with shortness of breath, palpitations, chest pain, a choking sensation, and feeling of impending doom. She said she had a hard time driving a car, especially on the highways, and was now driving exclusively on narrow, well-protected, low-speed sidestreets. This increased greatly the time it took for her to get home or to work, but she did not mind.

Three months later, with no specific treatment, her symptoms had subsided. She no longer had any nightmares and had only occasional trepidation when she had to go by speeding cars. She had basically resumed her usual activities and had dissuaded the lawyer from any further legal activity.

Resiliency and Anxiety

Given the variety and complexity of anxiety pictures, one may ask whether they are produced exclusively by environmental events or by genetic factors.

Dr. Michael Rutter (1985) has addressed this matter in relation to emotional disorders in general. Individual differences in response to acute life events has suggested the existence of vulnerability factors that increase susceptibility to stressors and of buffering influences that serve a protective function in the same circumstances. Whether a person suffers the illness may be determined by interaction between vulnerability and resiliency. "The patterning of stresses, individual differences caused by both constitutional and experiential factors, compensating experiences outside the home, the development of self-esteem, the scope and range of available opportunities, and appropriate degree of structure and control, the availability of personal bonds and intimate relationships, and the acquisition of coping skills" may explain how people may be protected from suffering illness in the presence of stress. Stress itself may not be the only determinant of illness; other preceding and concurrent circumstances may be major factors. The promotion of resiliency may not lie in the avoidance of stress but in encountering it in a way that allows self-confidence and social competence to increase through mastery and appropriate responsibility. Dr. Rutter's work has suggested a complex interaction among many factors, including the individual's genetic endowment and the stresses he or she may face. Such interaction may produce or prevent mental illness.

References

American Psychiatric Association. *Diagnostic and Statistical Manual of Mental Disorders.* 3rd ed. Washington, D.C.: *American Psychiatric Association*, 1980.
Goodwin, D. W. *Anxiety.* New York: Oxford University Press, 1986.
Rutter, M. "Resilience in the Face of Adversity: Protective Factors and Resistance to Psychiatric Disorder." *British Journal of Psychiatry,* 1985, *147,* 598–611.

Rodrigo A. Muñoz is associate professor of clinical psychiatry at the University of California at San Diego, president of the American Academy of Clinical Psychiatrists, and president of the Western Mood and Sleep Disorders Instutute in San Diego.

Anxiety is ubiquitous, but anxiety disorders and their distribution can be studied following the tenets of medical epidemiology. The differential diagnosis of anxiety disorders is a most taxing discipline. This chapter presents the problems involved and several realistic solutions.

The Epidemiology of Anxiety

James Reich

When someone speaks of fears or anxieties without describing a specific situation, we often think of persons with emotional problems—as if healthy persons would never have these feelings. But this is not the case. Fears and anxieties are part of the normal pattern of development. It is normal for children between the ages of two and six to develop a fear of strangers. This fear later resolves. It is reported that of children in the five-to-fourteen-year-old age group, only 5 percent would not admit to having any fears at all. In short, some fears are part of the healthy developmental path of childhood. Fears are very common in childhood but tend to disappear with age; even in clinical populations, the earlier the onset of the fear, the greater the probability of spontaneous remission.

In adults also, fear and anxieties have an integral role in adaptation and health. A small amount of performance anxiety can actually aid in the performance of a task. The fear generated by a life-threatening situation can provide the stimulus necessary for one to act to save oneself.

In what situations, then, are fears and anxieties no longer in the realm of the normal? Fears become an emotional problem when the responses they evoke become consistently maladaptive. This can be due either to a reaction that is in excess of the demands of the situation or to

---

I would like to acknowledge the assistance of R. Noyes, M.D., and R. Crowe, M.D., in the preparation of this manuscript.

R. A. Muñoz (ed.). *Treating Anxiety Disorders.*
New Directions for Mental Health Services, no. 32. San Francisco: Jossey-Bass, Winter 1986.

extensive avoidance of some important life situations, either of which causes a decrease in the quality of life. These maladaptive responses are beyond voluntary control, and sufferers usually realize that their fears are unreasonable. These maladaptive fear responses can be either cognitive-emotional or physiological or both. The physiological response can be rapid heartbeat, hyperventilation, sweating, flushing, a feeling of tightness in the chest, or related symptoms. The cognitive symptoms may consist of fears of dying, losing control, or being in a situation where help is not available, or general feelings of extreme apprehension. When such consistently maladaptive reactions persist for prolonged periods of time without documented physical illness and occur in other than life-threatening situations, fears and/or anxiety have become maladaptive.

These syndromes have long been recognized by clinicians and in literature. Hippocrates (unknown date) described two phobic subjects, Burton (1621) described an anxiety neurosis, and Shakespeare described a cat phobia in the *Merchant of Venice*. Some of the many names under which such syndromes have been described in the past include "muscular exhaustion of the heart," irritable heart, DaCosta's syndrome, cardiac neurosis, neurocirculatory asthenia, nervous exhaustion, and anxiety neurosis. (There are many other names as well.) The different names reflect to some extent the different theories of etiology entertained. These have ranged from defective cardiac function to unresolved unconscious psychic conflicts.

The different names and definitions these syndromes have had in the past have often made it difficult to accurately diagnose and study them. They do, however, fall into broad, but not mutually exclusive, categories. These are single fears (or phobias) that do not generalize to other situations; complexes of fears or anxieties that highly restrict lifestyles and functioning; and sudden attacks of panic that often are not precipitated by a specific event.

Prevalence of Anxiety Disorders

The incidence of a disorder is the number of new cases arising in a given time period per unit of population; the prevalence is the number of disorders per unit population present at a given time. There are many problems involved in the collection and interpretation of both incidence and prevalence information. One is that unless a disorder is exceedingly common, it is often impractical to perform an incidence study. Unless the disorder occurs frequently, a properly performed incidence study would require following large numbers of healthy subjects for a long period of time in order to identify a few new cases. This is often expensive and impractical. As a result, most studies are prevalence studies. If a disorder is of long duration and new cases are relatively rare (such as agoraphobia or panic disorder), then the findings of prevalence studies do begin to approximate incidence. If the duration of an illness is of short duration, however (as are many phobias), the two types of estimates may differ greatly.

There are other problems in estimating prevalence. One is that different investigators often use different diagnostic criteria. Another is that prevalence differs according to the type of group sampled. There are basically three types of group samples: inpatients, outpatients, and community survey. The community survey gives the best estimate of the overall prevalence of a disorder, although the other estimates are useful to clinicians and for estimation of service needs. In disorders where treatment is frequently sought, the prevalence increases in outpatient and inpatient settings. However, in diseases such as phobias, where treatment is not frequently sought, the prevalence may be higher in the community. Given these limitations, let me review informed estimates for the various anxiety disorders.

Phobias. Estimates of the prevalence of phobias range from 39 percent (social phobia in a group of outpatient-treatment alcoholics, Smail and others [1984]) to a community estimate of .05 percent (Hollingshead and Redlich [1958]). Probably the best current estimates for DSM-III-defined phobia are provided by Robins and others (1984) for lifetime prevalence and Weissman and others (1984) for six-month prevalence. Both of these studies were based on a carefully selected community random sample consisting of over 3,000 informants. (This was part of the Epidemiologic Catchment Area [ECA] Study sponsored by the NIMH.) These studies used the same diagnostic instruments (National Institute of Mental Health Diagnostic Interview Schedule [NIMH-DIS]) and achieved adequate cross-site reliability. For the New Haven, Baltimore, and St. Louis sites, total lifetime phobias ranged from 7.8 percent (New Haven) to 33.3 percent (Baltimore). (Lifetime here refers to an informant's having had the disorder sometime during the course of his or her life but not necessarily having it at the time of the interview.) For six-month prevalence Weissman (1984) reports an approximate average of 1.3 percent for males and 1.7 percent for females for social phobia, and 4.3 percent for males and 7.0 percent for females for simple phobia. (These are average estimates as once again there is intersite variation.) Virtually all the observations on phobia note a preponderance of females. A reasonable minimal estimate would be that the female:male ratio in phobias is at least 2:1.

As this wide range of estimates indicates, phobia is an especially difficult disorder to measure. One reason for this is the relatively low interrater reliability of the DIS when measuring phobia. Robins and others (1981) report a kappa of .47 for interrater reliability for simple phobia. This is relatively low. A reason for this low reliability may be that phobia can be an easy disorder to conceal from friends and acquaintances. As most people are reluctant to admit to a disability they need not publicize, some may not have admitted it to interviewers, and this may have had some effect on the diversity of results found. It is also difficult to judge impairment appropriately. For example, if someone has a fear of heights

Table 1. DMS-III Definitions of Anxiety Disorders

I. **Agoraphobia**

A. The individual has a marked fear of and thus avoids being alone or in public places from which escape might be difficult or help not available in case of sudden incapacitation, e.g., crowds, tunnels, bridges, public transportation.
B. There is increasing constriction of normal activities until the fears or avoidance behavior dominate the individual's life.
C. Not due to major depressive episode, obsessive-compulsive disorder, paranoid personality disorder, or schizophrenia.

II. **Simple Phobia**

A. Persistent irrational fear of and compelling desire to avoid an object or situation other than being alone or in public places away from home (agoraphobia), or of humiliation or embarrassment in certain social situations (social phobia). Phobic objects are often animals, and phobic situations frequently involve heights or closed spaces.
B. Significant distress from the disturbance and the recognition by the individual that his or her fear is excessive or unreasonable.
C. Not due to another mental disorder.

III. **Social Phobia**

A. Persistent irrational fear of and compelling desire to avoid a situation where an individual is exposed to possible scrutiny by others and fears that he or she may act in a way that will be humiliating or embarrassing.
B. Significant distress from the disturbance and the recognition by the individual that his or her fear is excessive or unreasonable.
C. Not due to another mental disorder.

IV. **Panic Disorder**

A. At least three panic attacks within a three-week period in circumstances other than during marked physical exertion or in a life-threatening situation. The attacks are not precipitated only by exposure to a circumscribed phobic stimulus.
B. Panic attacks are manifested by discrete periods of apprehension or fear, and at least four of the following symptoms appear during each attack: (1) dyspnea, (2) palpitation, (3) chest pain or discomfort, (4) choking or smothering sensation, (5) dizziness or vertigo, (6) feelings of unreality, (7) paresthesias (tingling in hands or feet), (8) hot and cold flashes, (9) sweating, (10) faintness, (11) trembling or shaking, (12) fear of dying, going crazy, or doing something uncontrolled during an attack.
C. Not due to a physical disorder or another mental disorder.

V. **Generalized Anxiety Disorder**

A. Generalized, persistent anxiety is manifested by symptoms from three of the following four categories:

1. Motor tension: shakiness, jitteriness, jumpiness, trembling, tension, muscles aches, fatigability, inability to relax, eyelid twitch, furrowed brow, strained face, fidgeting, restlessness, easy startle
2. Autonomic hyperactivity: sweating, heart pounding or racing, cold clammy hands, dry mouth, dizziness, light-headedness, paresthesias, upset stomach, hot or cold spells, frequent urination, diarrhea, discomfort in the pit of the stomach, lump in the throat, flushing, pallor, high resting pulse and respiration rate

Table 1. *(continued)*

3. Apprehensive expectation: anxiety, worry, fear, rumination, and anticipation of misfortune to self or others
4. Vigilance and scanning: hyperattentiveness resulting in distractibility, difficulty in concentrating, insomnia, feeling "on edge," irritability, impatience.

B. The anxious mood has been continous for at least one month.

C. Not due to another mental disorder, such as a depressive disorder or schizophrenia.

D. The individual is at least eighteen years of age.

VI. **Post-Traumatic Stress Disorder**

A. Existence of a recognizable stressor that would evoke significant symptoms of distress in almost anyone.

B. Re-experiencing of the trauma as evidenced by at least one of the following:

1. Recurrent and intrusive recollections of the event
2. Recurrent dreams of the event
3. Sudden acting or feeling as if the traumatic event were reoccurring, because of an association with an environmental or ideational stimulus.

C. Numbing of responsiveness to, or reduced involvement with, the external world, beginning some time after the trauma, as shown by at least one of the following:

1. Markedly diminished interest in one or more significant activities
2. Feeling of detachment or estrangement from others
3. Constricted affect.

D. At least two of the following symptoms that were not present before the trauma:

1. Hyperalertness or exaggerated startle response
2. Sleep disturbance
3. Guilt about surviving when others have not, or about behavior required for survival
4. Memory impairment or trouble concentrating
5. Avoidance of activities that arouse recollection of the traumatic event
6. Intensification of symptoms by exposure to events that symbolize or resemble the traumatic event.

but in the course of his or her life is never required to be in high places, do they have a phobia? Nonetheless, from informants who did admit to having the disorder, phobia is the most frequent emotional disorder in women in all age groups, and one of the most common in men as well.

Agoraphobia. In the past the prevalence of agoraphobia has been variously estimated at between 1 and 4 percent of the community population. The ECA estimate of lifetime prevalence ranges from 5.3 to 12.5 percent in females and from 1.5 to 5.2 percent in males (depending on the site). The six-month ECA prevalences range from 2.7 to 5.8 percent in women and from 0.9 to 3.4 percent in men. As in other phobias, there is a female preponderance in agoraphobia in both lifetime and six-month prevalence at all sites; a female:male ratio of 2:1 would be a conservative estimate. (In DSM-IIIR the categories of panic disorder and agoraphobia will be combined [Spitzer and Williams, 1983].)

Panic Disorder. There are several reasonable estimates of panic disorder prior to the ECA studies. Kannel and Dawber (1958), using the Framingham study data diagnosed 10.8 percent of that population as having neurocirculatory asthenia. Wheeler and others (1950) estimated that 6 percent of 2,799 private cardiology patients had the same disease. Weissman and others (1978), in a community sample of 511 in New Haven, Connecticut, using the Schedule for Affective Disorders and Schizophrenia (SADS) with Research Diagnostic Criteria (RDC), observed a point prevalence of 0.4 percent. Dean and others (1983), in a study to compare various diagnostic systems, observed a 0.7 percent community prevalence rate. The ECA lifetime estimates of panic range from 1.6 to 2.1 percent in females and from 0.6 to 1.2 percent in males. ECA six-month prevalences range from 0.6 to 1.0 percent in women and from 0.3 to 0.8 percent in men. A female:male estimate of 1.5–2.0:1 appears reasonable.

Generalized Anxiety. There are several good estimates of generalized anxiety disorder prior to the ECA study. Weissman and others (1978), in a community study, estimated a point prevalence of 2.6 percent (using RDC); Uhlenhuth and others (1983), using a symptom checklist on 3,161 community sample interviews, estimated a one-year prevalence of 6.4 percent; Dean and others (1983), in a community survey of 576 women (using the CATEGO diagnostic system), estimated a 2.6 percent prevalence. The ECA initial reports do not mention generalized anxiety as an individual diagnosis. Uhlenhuth reports a female:male ratio of 2:1.

Post-Traumatic Stress Disorder. If there is one anxiety disorder with a large environmental component, it is post-traumatic stress disorder; it is largely environmentally determined. This may be one reason why even in the relatively discrete group of Vietnam veterans there are disagreements about its exact prevalence (Figley 1978; Kolb, 1984; LaGuardia and others, 1983; and Borus, 1974). As a result, specific prevalence rates for different population groups are not available. The disorder does exist, however, and should be looked for in populations exposed to extreme stress.

It is unclear exactly how much the prevalence of anxiety disorders would change over time. One report (Murphy and others, 1984) notes an amazing stability of prevalence for anxiety disorders over a twelve-year period in a community population. Several follow-up studies of agoraphobia indicate stability of the diagnosis over time (Marks and Lader, 1973; Errera and Coleman, 1963; Agras and others, 1969; Roberts, 1964). The ECA study (Robins and others, 1984) gives indications for a possible increase in prevalence in some of the younger age groups. The rough prevalences probably can be considered reasonably stable, although the issue is not entirely resolved. The many technical difficulties involved in determining stability of prevalence include changes in populations over time and changes in measurement instruments or criteria. When retrospective information is used (such as lifetime prevalence for which one is relying on an informant's memory), there are problems of accurate recall. It should also be remembered that these diagnostic categories are not mutually exclusive. For example, panic disorder coexists extensively with agoraphobia and not uncommonly with phobias and generalized anxiety as well. As a result, these prevalences are not often additive.

The classic description of the relationship to social class and mental disorders is that of Hollingshead and Redlich (1958). In their book they use the diagnosis of phobic anxiety reaction, which is hard to translate into DSM-III diagnoses. Nonetheless, they found an increased and inverse relationship between social class and phobic anxiety reaction. Proportionately more anxiety disorders were found in the upper social classes than would be expected by chance. More recently, Himmelfarb and Murrell (1984) note a similar finding in their examination of the correlates of anxiety in older (over fifty five years) adults. However, the bulk of the recent literature shows no consistent relationship between anxiety disorders and social class.

Course of Illness

Single Phobias. The prognosis for isolated simple or social phobias, although not well documented, appears fairly good. Phobias of this type have the potential of spontaneous remission and are well treated by behavioral techniques. Simple phobias in childhood and younger ages have an especially good chance of remission. There is evidence, at least in children, that even highly disruptive single phobias will tend to resolve without long-term negative sequelae (Cummings, 1944, 1946).

Panic Attacks. Marks and Lader (1973), in reviewing the data on the course of panic attacks up to that time, came to conclude that 41 to 59 percent of cases were recovered or much improved at a one- to twenty-year follow-up (depending on the particular study). They were of the opinion that roughly 50 percent of these cases had a satisfactory outcome. They were not able to determine any firm prognostic variables. Because the studies reviewed utilized treatment that would today in all likelihood be considered ineffective (such as rest and sedatives, or four to seven psychotherapy sessions) these studies could be considered to provide information about untreated patients. Errera and Coleman (1963) performed a long follow-up (average twenty-three years) on 19 patients seen at the Grace New Haven Community Hospital in the years 1937–1940. They found 63 percent virtually unchanged, with a further 17 percent severe morbidity. It is unclear how much this differs from Marks and Lader's conclusions, since their 60 percent attrition rate on follow-up could well have biased their sample.

Wheeler and others (1950) performed a twenty-year follow-up on 173 patients diagnosed as having neurocirculatory asthenia. The criteria were roughly similar to those used for panic disorder in DSM-III. Of the 173, 171 were located, and of these 11.7 percent were well, 73.3 percent had symptoms but mild or no disability, and 15 percent had symptoms of a moderate to severe degree of difficulty. This group appeared to have an especially benign course, and it is possible that the criteria for diagnosis were not as stringent as those found in the DSM-III for panic disorders.

Noyes and Clancy (1976) followed up after five years 57 patients, 82 percent of the original group with anxiety neurosis seen on a psychiatric consultation service. At the follow-up period 16 percent were unimpaired and 51 percent were mildly impaired. The women in the study showed a more favorable outcome than the men. Age at time of contact was a predictor of outcome in men (the older the age of onset, the worse the outcome) but not in women.

Another important follow-up finding on anxiety and physical illness contributed by Noyes and others (1978) was a six-year follow-up of a separate group of patients with panic attacks seen on a psychiatric consultation service (N-112) and compared them to matched surgical controls (N-110). Patients with panic disorders reported more episodes of illness and hospitalizations, even when episodes due to anxiety were excluded. Also significant was the finding that the anxiety group (as documented in chart information using blood pressure, hypertension treatment, and X-ray confirmation of ulcers) had significantly more peptic ulcers and hypertension than controls.

Coryell and others (1982) and Coryell (1984) followed up 113 former panic patients thirty-five years after index admission and compared their mortality rates with those of depressives. (Depressives are known to have a higher mortality rate than the general population.) They found no difference between the overall mortality of depressives and panic patients. Compared to normals, patients with panic disorder had an excess of mortality in the last decade of follow-up ($p<.001$). This trend was stronger in men than women. Men with panic disorder had an excess number of deaths due to circulatory system disease. The suicide rates for the depressed and panic patients were equivalent. Although Wheeler and others (1950) did not find differential mortality in follow-up of their population, the generally more benign course of that group appears to indicate that they were less severely ill than patients studied by Coryell.

A summary of these findings is that over a long period of follow-up it would not be unreasonable to expect to see 50 to 70 percent of anxiety patients (panic and generalized anxiety) show some amount of improvement. Total remissions, however, are much less common. There may be some increased risk for peptic ulcer and hypertension in panic disorder patients, as well as higher mortality rates, higher suicide rates, and a larger number of deaths due to circulatory disease.

Agoraphobia. There are several follow-up studies of agoraphobia. Roberts (1964) followed up 41 "house-bound housewives" for periods ranging from one to sixteen years (most over five years). He found 55.3 percent improved on follow-up, although virtually all the improved still had some residual symptoms. Cohen and others (1984) followed up at two years on 40 of 45 patients in a study comparing imipramine to placebo and relaxation to exposure therapy. There were no differences among treatment and two-thirds of all patients were improved or much improved. Emmelkamp and Kuipers (1979), using behavior therapy on 70 patients, and Meyer and Gelder (1963), using psychotherapy on 5, report 75 percent and 60 percent improvement at four- and one-year follow-ups, respectively. Munby and Johnston (1980) report that gains made with behavior therapy at six months tend to persist at five- to nine-year follow-up. Agras and others (1972) followed up a group of 30 untreated phobics identified by a community survey technique using a fear checklist. In adults he found 43 percent improved or recovered, 20 percent unchanged, and 33 percent worse at five-year follow up. Overall, it can be estimated that 50 to 70 percent of agoraphobics will have diminution of symptoms at long-term follow-up. It should be noted that the follow-up studies reported here involved treatment, and an untreated population might fare worse. It should also be remembered that many of the improved still have significant symptoms.

Age of Onset. There are two good reports on the age of onset of anxiety disorders. Sheehan and others (1981) reported on 162 cases of anxiety disorder seen at a psychiatric outpatient clinic. They divided the disorders into exogenous (N=62, roughly the equivalent of DSM-III simple and social phobias) and endogenous ($N = 100$, roughly the equivalent to DSM-III panic attacks, agoraphobia, and generalized anxiety disorders). Endogenous and exogenous disorders had a mean onset of 24.1 years (S.D. 8.9) and 19.7 years (S.D. 12.8) respectively. The ages of onset of these two groups are significantly different ($p. < .01$).

Thyer and others (1985), studying 423 psychiatric outpatients, found findings consistent with Sheehan's. They found the following mean ages of onset: simple phobia, 16.1 (S.D. = 13.0); social phobia, 15.7 (S.D. = 8.5); panic disorder, 26.6 (S.D. = 11.5); agoraphobia with panic attacks, 26.3 (S.D. = 9.1); agoraphobia without panic attacks, 27.5 (S.D. = 7.8); and generalized anxiety disorder, 22.8 (S.D. = 12.0). Simple and social phobias did not differ significantly from each other; however, both were significantly lower than all other ages of onset, with the exception of generalized anxiety disorder.

It appears from these two reports that there are two ages of onset for the anxiety disorders. These two studies are also in agreement with the findings of Anderson and others (1984) on the age of onset of panic and generalized anxiety disorder. Simple and social phobia appear to occur in mid- to late adolescence, whereas panic, generalized anxiety, and agoraphobia appear to occur in the middle twenties. In general, only the unusual anxiety disorders will present with an onset after age forty.

Etiology of Anxiety Disorders

Family and Genetic Studies. It is well established that hereditary or familial factors often play a role in some emotional illnesses such as depression. There is evidence for a role of familial factors in anxiety disorders as well. Marks (1969) reviews literature that demonstrates that anxiety traits can be bred in animals. For example, in just three or four generations mice can be bred to have a significant amount of genetically determined "anxious" behavior. In human twin studies, Slater and Shields (1969) found that for "anxiety states," 50 percent of the monozygotic co-twins showed concurrent anxiety disorders, whereas only 2 to 3 percent of the dizygotic co-twins did so. Torgersen's (1983) results were very similar to those of Slater and Shields.

Most interesting are the family studies examining the transmission of agoraphobia or panic attacks. Burns and Thorpe (1977) and Burns (1980), examining the older literature, find a high incidence of anxiety neurosis in the families of anxiety neurosis probands. The best recent literature, however, comes from the Iowa group. Noyes and others (1978) performed a family history study on 112 patients diagnosed as anxiety neurotics. The morbidity risk of anxiety among first-degree relatives was 18 percent for neurotics and 3 percent among controls. Relatives were also found to be at higher risk for alcoholism. Crowe and others (1983) performed a family interview study on 278 first-degree relatives of 41 probands with DSM-III panic disorder and compared them to a similar number of relatives from controls. The rate of definite and probable panic disorder was 24.7 percent in panic relatives and 2.2 percent in control relatives. Harris and others (1983) performed a study comparing the morbid risk of first-degree relatives in agoraphobia patients, panic patients, and controls. The morbid risk for all anxiety disorders was 32 percent for relatives of agoraphobics, 33 percent for panic relatives, and 15 percent for relatives of controls. Relatives of agoraphobics were also found to be at higher risk for alcohol disorders. In both the Crowe and Harris studies females were at higher risk. It is fairly clear at this point that panic and agoraphobic patients have a higher familial risk for anxiety disorders than nonanxiety patients. It is likely there is a higher risk for alcoholism as well. What form the genetic transmission takes and whether agoraphobia, panic, and generalized anxiety assort separately is a question for future research. The most recent family work by Noyes and others (in press), however, supports the position that agoraphobia is merely a more severe variant of panic disorder.

Additional indirect evidence for a genetic hypothesis comes from reports indicating that biochemical abnormalities are associated with panic attacks. Several researchers have shown that lactate infusion or CO2 inhalation is a precipitant of panic attacks in those with the disorder but not in those without the disorder (Rainey and others, 1984; Leibowitz and others, 1984; Gorman and others, 1984).

Environmental Influences on the Development of Anxiety Disorder. There is no doubt that in some circumstances fear or anxiety responses can be largely learned behavior. The clearest example is post-traumatic stress disorder. Here specific traumatic events (usually life-threatening) result in ongoing fears related to that specific situation. Work with these disorders in former soldiers reveals that these symptoms can be self-sustaining and fairly long-term (Kolb, 1984; Merbaum, 1977; Figley, 1978).

In disorders such as agoraphobia and panic disorder, which are largely familial and presumably biochemical, environmental events may have a preciptitating or aggravating role. It is not uncommon for patients with panic attacks to relate the period of onset to a time when they were under a severe stress. Although this is retrospective data and anecdotal, it is also possible that in those with an underlying predisposition, a severe environmental stress might trigger the disease process. For those with existing anxiety disorders, it is clear that increased environmental stress or conflict may well exacerbate existing symptoms. It has been reported (Buglass and others, 1977) that for some women with anxiety disorders, symptoms may get worse premenstrually.

Simple and social phobias probably fall between post-traumatic stress disorder and panic and agoraphobia in terms of genetic and environmental influences. Although the environmental precipitants in these disorders are not so severe as to constitute an explanation in themselves, there is still considerable room for learning theory to explain much about these disorders. Wolpe (1981) and Öst and Hugdahl (1981) provide good discussions of the learning theory evidence.

Cultural influences are also present in anxiety disorders. The cultural influence, however, appears to affect the way in which the disorder is expressed and not the presence or absence of the core symptoms of the disorder. Ndetei and Vadher (1984), using the CATEGO system to examine the presence of psychiatric diagnosis across nine cultural groups, found that although there was some variation, the CATEGO syndrome of general anxiety was present in roughly 10 to 15 percent for practically all cultures. The cultures examined were English, African, Jamaican, Continental European, English-speaking non-European, Asian, Middle Eastern, Far Eastern, and Caribbean. Other reports from Kenya (Dhadphale and others, 1983) and Transkei (Gijana, 1981) appear consistent with the thesis that anxiety disorders exist in all cultures. So, although occasionally one culture will present in a radically different way (such as Koro found only among the Malay) the core anxiety disorders are transcultural phenomena.

Nosology of Anxiety Disorders. Marks in 1970 classified phobic disorders as animal phobias, the agoraphobic syndrome, and social phobias. Agoraphobic syndrome is roughly equivalent in DSM-III terms to panic disorder, agoraphobia, and generalized anxiety. The division seems to have stood the test of time fairly well. These groups have different ages of onset, different clinical courses, and different responses to treatment. Noyes and others most recent family study (in press) indicates that agoraphobia is most likely merely a more severe variant of panic disorder, and the DSM-IIIR may combine these two categories.

The Relationship Between Anxiety and Depression

A question of clinical, theoretical, and therapeutic importance is that of the relationship between the affective and the anxiety disorders. One approach has been to use factor analytic techniques to determine whether anxiety patients can be discriminated from depressed patients in that fashion. This route led to successful differentiation of the two disorders by several groups (Derogatis and others, 1972; Prusoff and Klerman, 1974; Mountjoy and Roth, 1982).

A second route to determine distinctions between the two sets of disorders has been to follow the course of the illness. Several groups have been able to show a consistently worse outcome for anxiety disorders as compared to depression (Schapira and others, 1972; Kerr and others, 1972; Gurney and others, 1972; Coryell and others, 1983). Coryell and others (1983) not only found a higher rate of recovery at five years for unipolar depressives (60.2 percent) than for patients with panic disorder (15.5 percent) but also found that the two groups had no predictors of outcome in common.

This is not to say that anxiety and depressive symptoms are not found together. In reality they often coexist. Clancy and others (1978), in following 112 patients diagnosed as anxiety neurotics, found that 44 percent reported an episode of secondary depression, compared to only 7 percent of control patients. These and other similar findings have even led some investigators to question whether the dichotomy between the two disorders should be rigidly observed. Van Valkenburg and others (1984), after comparing on a number of variables primary panic patients, panic patients with secondary depression, depression patients with secondary panic, and depressives, conclude that the category of "anxious depression" has validity and should be retained. Lechman and others (1983) and Weissman and others (1984), examining the familial relationships of patients with anxiety disorders and depression, found that first-degree relatives of probands having both depression and an anxiety disorder (panic attacks or agoraphobia) had higher risks for both anxiety disorders and depression than relatives of probands with depression alone. Breier and others (1984), in reviewing the temporal relationship among depression, agoraphobia, and panic, believe that in a subgroup of patients there is a common diathesis for anxiety and depressive disorder. Nystrom and Lindegard (1975), in a prospective study, found no premorbid personality differences in people who later become clinically depressed or anxious.

A reasonable middle position to take would be that first, in many cases anxiety and depressive disorders can be distinguished by symptom complex and course of illness. Second, prominent anxiety symptoms in depression or depressive symptoms in anxiety should be noted, as they may indicate prognosis or dictate treatment modalities. Third, patients with relatives suffering from both anxiety and depressive disorders are at especially high risk for both disorders and have a poor prognosis.

Personality and Anxiety

Anxiety patients tend to be reported to have had higher scores on anxiety-proneness and neuroticism than normals and depressives. Anxiety patients also tend to have higher scores on extroversion. However, recovered anxiety patients and recovered depressed patients do not differ on many personality tests, although both do differ from normals in that they have less emotional strength and are more interpersonally dependent and less extroverted. It appears that effects of state anxiety and state depression on many personality measures are similar. Murray and Blackburn (1974), using Cattell's 16 PF, found similarities between their unrecovered anxiety group and their recovered and unrecovered unipolar depressive group. Nystrom and Lindegard (1975), in a large prospective study using the Sjobring personality factors, were unable to show any differences in the premorbid personalities of those who later became depressed and those who later became anxious. Tyrer and others (1983) noted that passive-dependent personalities were linked to anxiety neurosis and phobic neurosis; however, this did not distinguish anxiety from depressive patients. Alternatively, Gurney and others (1972) noted increased neurotic traits in childhood in anxious as opposed to depressed patients, while Roth and others (1972) found an increased incidence of personality disorder in anxious as opposed to depressed patients.

In sum, it appears that there may be some characteristic premorbid personality traits in anxiety patients; however, in the normal course of events state anxiety makes them difficult to evaluate. These premorbid traits apparently are similar in many ways to those found in depressives. It is interesting to note that in their study of 1200 agoraphobics in Britain,

Marks and Herst (1970) noted that the most important features characterizing phobics who never saw a physician were personality traits: increased social timidity and difficulty confiding in other people.

Treatment

The treatment of anxiety disorders, as of other emotional disorders, does not always reach everyone in need, and those reached do not always receive optimum treatment. Agras and others (1969) estimated that 57 in 1000 people have seen a physician about a severe fear or phobia, but only 9 in 1000 received active treatment. Hollingshead and Redlich's (1958) estimates for those in adequate treatment were even lower. Judging from the prevalence estimates of the ECA study, this population is probably undertreated. This is consistent with what patients themselves believe. Burns and Thorpe (1977), working with data from the National Survey of Agoraphobics, found that 73.8 percent felt they had not received adequate help for their agoraphobia. In a study of psychotherapeutic drug usage, Uhlenhuth and others (1983) found that 55 percent of agoraphobics, 27 percent of generalized anxiety patients, and 12 percent of other phobics used an antianxiety agent, although many only used these medications intermittently. Eight percent of agoraphobics used antidepressant agents. Forty-one percent of agoraphobics, 79 percent of other phobics, and 62 percent of generalized anxiety patients used no psychotherapeutic agent at all.

As in all other disorders, the key to appropriate treatment is proper diagnosis. Anxiety patients often present with physical complaints (Clancy and Noyes, 1976; Katon, 1984). However, if anxiety symptoms are present, medical illness must be ruled out, since some medical disorders, such as thyrotoxicosis, cardiac arrythmias, pheochromocytomas, and multiple sclerosis, may present with similar symptoms. For a newly presenting patient a good history, a thyroid panel, and a recent EKG would seem a reasonable screen. Next it must be ascertained whether the symptoms are clearly secondary to some primary emotional disorder, such as schizophrenia or depression. In this case the best results will come from treating the primary disorder. After a specific anxiety diagnosis is established, specific treatment plans can be considered.

There are basically two treatment approaches to the anxiety disorders; behavioral and pharmacologic. The best known behavioral technique is systematic desensitization, which may or may not be combined with relaxation training. This works in the following way: First, the patients learn relaxation techniques. Then the patient develops a personal hierarchy of feared situations (from least to most threatening). Utilizing relaxation and imagery of increasingly difficult situations in the hierarchy, the patient gradually learns to tolerate feared situations—first in imagery and later in practice. Other behavioral techniques that have received trials at various times include hypnosis, flooding (implosion therapy), paradoxical intention, cognitive manipulation, and operant conditioning techniques, to name a few. It is now evident that the key factor in behavior treatment is in vivo exposure—direct exposure to the feared stimulus (Mathews and others, 1981; Emmelkamp, 1982).

Pharmacologic treatments available include monoamine oxidase inhibitors such as phenelzine and tricyclic antidepressants such as imipramine. These are often effective for panic attacks, although not generally accepted as effective for generalized anxiety. Alprazolam (Xanax) and the benzodiazapines (Valium, Librium, etc.) appear to be effective for treating panic attacks, with some help for intercurrent anxiety as well. Some beta-2-blocker drugs such as propranolol that inhibit the physiologic expression of panic symptoms have been helpful in some cases as well.

Both the behavioral and pharmacologic treatments have been shown to be effective in helping certain patients, with some evidence of gains from behavioral techniques being maintained during long-term followup. Which treatments are used depends on the patients and the specific disorder. Simple or social phobias will likely respond well to behavioral approaches alone, although pharmacotherapy may be used briefly as an adjunct. In generalized anxiety, agoraphobia, and panic disorders, although behavior techniques alone can be successful in reducing symptoms, often many residual symptoms and morbidity are present after improvement. As a result, most physicians feel that a combined behavioral and pharmacologic approach is the best route with these patients. Post-traumatic stress syndrome is the only specific disorder in which counseling techniques may be the main thrust of treatment, although even here pharmacologic adjuncts may be useful. The nonphysician mental health professional also has an important role to play in the treatment of these patients, as is described in the next section.

An important concern of treatment is the association of alcoholism with anxiety states. Clinicians are familiar with anxiety patients who use alcohol to reduce anxiety when they must go into a feared situation and are aware of the potential of alcohol dependence developing. Woodruff and others (1972) reported an anxiety neurotic population drawn from a psychiatry outpatient clinic ($N = 62$) in which 50 percent had a secondary alcohol dependency and 14.5 percent had a diagnosis of alcoholism. Smail and others (1984) found that over half of the alcoholics they interviewed had symptoms of either agoraphobia or social phobia when last drinking. Winokur and Holemon (1963), in a cross-sectional study found that 5 of 31 anxiety neurotic outpatients had difficulties with alcohol abuse. Katon (1984) found that 24 percent of his sample of 55 panic disorder patients had difficulty with alcohol abuse on dependence. There is also evidence of increased incidence of alcoholism in the families of agoraphobics (Munjack and Moss, 1981; Noyes and others, 1978; Harris and others, 1983).

Also relevant to treatment is the fact that other emotional illnesses (such as depression) may mimic anxiety states. If it is clear that anxiety symptoms are secondary to another emotional disorder, treatment should be instituted for the primary disorder. Conversely, anxiety disorders may mimic physical illness. Marks and Lader (1973) estimate that 10 percent of cardiology clinic patients are in fact anxiety patients. (Many of these patients actually do have benign minor cardiac abnormalities.)

Role of Social Workers and Mental Health Professionals

Nonphysician mental health workers have an important role to play in the diagnosis and treatment of anxiety disorders. This role derives from two factors. The first is that patients with anxiety disorders are often reluctant to admit their disability. (There are some cases in which the problem is not even known to a spouse.) Second, at least in panic attacks and agoraphobia, these illnesses are extremely demoralizing, and the patients find it hard to maintain the resolve to follow through on treatment plans. In many situations nonphysician mental health professionals spend more time with some patients than do physicians. This means they may be in a better position to discover symptoms of anxiety disorders in patients who are reluctant to reveal these symptoms. (Many of these patients have been informed by physicians in the past that it was "all in their head," since no organic cause could be found.)

Once identified, the treatment of these patients requires strong encouragement. Many patients feel they should "beat the problems on their own" and not engage in behavioral treatment or pharmacotherapy. Others who are ashamed of their illness may feel being a psychiatric patient a difficult stigma to tolerate. It is also hard to overestimate the demoralizing effect of having a severe panic attack early in the course of treatment. The mental health professional can help here in several ways. Education is a key factor. Patients are greatly helped by an understanding of the nature of their illness—especially by realizing that the symptoms are not a defect of character. Next, encouragement can be provided to help patients get through the difficult initial stages of treatment and in overcoming setbacks. Often it takes great encouragement to enter feared situations. Along this line, the professional can be a key person in activating social support. Often this is the spouse or other care-giver, who when properly educated can be a major support to treatment. Alternatively, it can be a more structured network, such as an agoraphobic support group. Certainly, without the education and support provided by care-givers many well-designed treatment programs will fail.

References

Agras, W. S., Chapin, H. N., and Oliveau, D. "The Natural History of Phobia." *Archives of General Psychiatry,* 1972, *26,* 315–317.

Agras, W. S., Sylvester, D., and Oliveau, D. "The Epidemiology of Common Fears and Phobias." *Comprehensive Psychiatry,* 1969, *10,* 151–156.

Anderson, D. J., Noyes, R., and Crowe, R. R. "A Comparison of Panic Disorder and Generalized Anxiety Disorder." *American Journal of Psychiatry,* 1984, *141,* 572–575.

Borus, J. "Incidence of Maladjustments in Vietnam Returnees." *Archives of General Psychiatry,* 1974, *30,* 554–557.

Breier, A., Charney, D. S., and Henninger, G. R. "Major Depression in Patients with Agoraphobia and Panic Disorder." *Archives of General Psychiatry,* 1984, *41,* 1129–1135.

Buglass, D., Clarke, J., Henderson, A. S., and others. "A Study of Agoraphobic Housewives." *Psychological Medicine,* 1977, *7,* 73–86.

Burns, L. E. "The Epidemiology of Fears and Phobias in General Practice." *Journal of Internal Medicine Research,* 1980 *8* (3), 1–7 (supplement).

Burns, L. E., and Thorpe, G. L. "Fears and Clinical Phobias: Epidemiologic Aspects and the National Survey of Agoraphobics." *Journal of Internal Medicine Research,* 1977, *5* (1), 132–139 (supplement).

Burton, R. *The Anatomy of Melancholy.* (11th ed.) Vol. 1. London, 1621, pp. 143–144.

Clancy, J., and Noyes, R. "Anxiety Neurosis: A Disease for the Medical Model." *Psychosomatics,* 1976, *17,* 90–93.

Clancy, J., Noyes, R., and others. "Secondary Depression in Anxiety Neurosis." *Journal of Nervous and Mental Disorder,* 1978, *166,* 846–856.

Cohen, S. P., Monteiro, W., and Marks, M. "Two-Year Follow-up of Agoraphobics after Exposure and Imipramine." *British Journal of Psychiatry,* 1984, *144,* 276–281.

Coryell, W. "Mortality After Thirty to Forty Years: Panic Disorder Compared with Other Psychiatric Illnesses." In L. Grinspoon (ed.), *Psychiatry Update,* American Psychiatric Association Annual Review, 1984, pp. 460–467.

Coryell, W., Noyes, R., and Clancy, J. "Excess Mortality in Panic Disorder: A Comparison with Primary Unipolar Depression." *Archives of General Psychiatry,* 1982, *39,* 701–703.

Coryell, W., Noyes, R., and Clancy, J. "Panic Disorder and Primary Unipolar Depression." *Journal of Affective Disorders,* 1983, *5,* 311–317.

Crowe, R. R., Noyes, R., Pauls, D. L., and others. "A Family Study of Panic Disorder." *Archives of General Psychiatry,* 1983, *40,* 1065–1069.

Cummings, J. D. "Incidence of Emotional Symptoms in School Children." *British Journal of Educational Psychology,* 1944, *15,* 151–161.

Cummings, J. D. "A Follow-up Study of Emotional Symptoms in School Children." *British Journal of Educational Psychology,* 1946, *16,* 163–177.

Dean, C., Surtees, P. G., and Sashidharan, S. P. "Comparison of Research Diagnostic System in an Edinburgh Community Sample." *British Journal of Psychiatry,* 1983, *142,* 247–256.

Derogatis, L. R., Lipman, R. S., Covi, L., and others. "Factorial Invariance of Symptom Dimensions in Anxious and Depressive Neurosis." *Archives of General Psychiatry,* 1972, *27,* 659–665.

Dhadphale, M., Ellison, R. H., and Griffin, L. "The Frequency of Psychiatric Disorders and Patients Attending Semi-Urban and Rural General Outpatient Clinics in Kenya." *British Journal of Psychiatry,* 1983, *142,* 379–383.

Emmelkamp, P.M.G. *Phobic and Obsessive-Compulsive Disorders.* New York: Plenum, 1982.

Emmelkamp, P.M.G., and Kuipers, A.C.M. "Agoraphobia: A Follow-up Study

Four Years After Treatment." *British Journal of Psychiatry,* 1979, *134,* 352-355.
Errera, P., and Coleman, J. V. "A Long-Term Follow-up Study of Neurotic Phobic Patients in a Psychiatric Clinic." *Journal of Nervous and Mental Disorders,* 1963, *136,* 267-271.
Figley, C. R. "Symptoms of Delayed Combat Stress Among a College Sample of Vietnam Veterans." *Military Medicine,* 1978, *143,* 107-110.
Gijana, E.W.M. "Psychiatric Disorders in a Developing Community as Reflected by Archival Material." *South African Medical Journal,* 1981, *59,* 988-991.
Gorman, J. M., Askanazi, J., Leibowitz, M. R., and others. "Response to Hyperventilation in a Group of Patients with Panic Disorder." *American Journal of Psychiatry,* 1984, *141,* 857-861.
Gurney, C., Roth, M., Garside, R. F., and others. "Studies in the Classification of Affective Disorders." *British Journal of Psychiatry,* 1972, *121,* 162-166.
Harris, E. L., Noyes, R., Crowe, R. R., and others. "Family Study of Agoraphobia." *Archives of General Psychiatry,* 1983, *40,* 1061-1064.
Himmelfarb, S., and Murrell, S. "The Prevelance and Correlates of Anxiety Symptoms in Older Adults." *Journal of Psychology,* 1984, *116,* 159-167.
Hippocrates. *On Epidemics V,* section LXXXII.
Hollingshead, A. B., and Redlich, F. C. *Social Class and Mental Illness: A Community Study.* New York: Wiley, 1958.
Kannel, W. B., and Dawber, T. R. "Neurocirculatory Asthenia." *Annals of Internal Medicine,* 1958, 1351-1360.
Katon, W. "Panic Disorder and Somatization: Review of 55 Cases." *American Journal of Medicine,* 1984, *77,* 101-106.
Kerr, T. A., Roth, M., Schapira, K., and others. "The Assessment and Prediction of Outcome in Affective Disorders." *British Journal of Psychiatry,* 1972, *121,* 167-174.
Kolb, L. C. "The Post-Traumatic Stress Disorders of Combat: A Subgroup with a Conditioned Emotional Response." *Military Medicine,* 1984, *149,* 237-243.
LaGuardia, R. L., Smith, G., Francois, R., and others. "Incidence of Delayed Stress Disorder Among Vietnam Era Veterans: The Effect of Priming on Response Set." *American Journal of Orthopsychiatry,* 1983, *53,* 18-26.
Lechman, J. F., Weissman, M. M., Merikangas, K. R., and others. "Panic Disorder and Major Depression." *Archives of General Psychiatry,* 1983, *40,* 1055-1061.
Leibowitz, M. R., Fyer, A., Gorman, J. M., and others. "Provocation of Panic Attacks by Sodium Lactate Infusion." *Journal of Clinical Psychiatry Monograph,* 1984, *2,* 18-20.
Marks, I. M. *Fears and Phobias.* New York: Academic Press, 1969.
Marks, I. M. "The Classification of Phobic Disorders." *British Journal of Psychiatry,* 1970, *116,* 377-386.
Marks, I. M., and Herst, E. R. "A Survey of 1,200 Agoraphobics in Britain." *Social Psychiatry,* 1970, *5,* 16-24.
Marks, I. M., and Lader, M. "Anxiety States (Anxiety Neurosis): A Review." *Journal of Nervous and Mental Disorders,* 1973, *156,* 3-18.
Mathews, A. M., Gelder, G., and Johnston, D. W. *Agoraphobia: Nature and Treatment.* New York: Guilford Press, 1981.
Merbaum, M. "Some Personality Characteristics of Soldiers Exposed to Extreme War Stress: A Follow-up of Post-Hospital Adjustments." *Journal of Clinical Psychology,* 1977, *33,* 558-562.
Meyer, V., and Gelder, M. G. "Follow-up of Agoraphobic Patients." *British Journal of Psychiatry,* 1963, *109,* 19-25.
Mountjoy, C. O., and Roth, M. "Studies in the Relationship Between Depressive

Disorders and Anxiety States." *Journal of Affective Disorders,* 1982, *4,* 127-147.
Munby, M., and Johnston, D. W. "Agoraphobia: The Long-Term Follow-up of Behavioral Treatment." *British Journal of Psychiatry,* 1980, *137,* 418-427.
Munjack, D. J., and Moss, H. B. "Affective Disorder and Alcoholism in Families of Agoraphobics." *Archives of General Psychiatry,* 1981, *38,* 869-871.
Murphy, J. M., Sobol, A. M., Neff, R. K., and others. "Stability of Prevalence: Depression and Anxiety Disorders." *Archives of General Psychiatry,* 1984, *41,* 990-997.
Murray, L. G., and Blackburn, I. M. "Personality Differences in Patients with Depressive Illness and Anxiety Neurosis." *Acta Psychiatrica Scandinavia,* 1974, *50,* 183-191.
Ndetei, D. M., and Vadher, A. "Pattern of Anxiety in a Cross-Cultural Hospital Population." *Acta Psychiatrica Scandinavia,* 1984, *70,* 69-72.
Noyes, R., and Clancy, J. "Anxiety Neurosis: A Five-Year Follow-up." *Journal of Nervous and Mental Disorders,* 1976, *162,* 200-205.
Noyes, R., Clancy, J., Crowe, R. R., and others. "The Familial Prevalence of Anxiety Neurosis." *Archives of General Psychiatry,* 1978, *35,* 1057-1059.
Noyes, R., Clancy, J., Hoenk, P. R., and others. "Anxiety Neurosis and Physical Illness." *Comprehensive Psychiatry,* 1978, *19,* 407-413.
Noyes, R., Crowe, R. R., Harris, E. L., and others. "Relationship Between Panic Disorder and Agoraphobia: A Family Study." *Archives of General Psychiatry,* in press.
Nystrom, S., and Lindegard B. "Predisposition for Mental Syndromes: A Study Comparing Predisposition for Depression, Neurasthenia, and Anxiety State." *Acta Psychiatric Scandinavia,* 1975, *51,* 69-76.
Öst, L., and Hugdahl, K. "Acquisition of Phobias and Anxiety Response Patterns in Clinical Patients." *Behavior Research and Therapy,* 1981, *19,* 439-447.
Prusoff, B., and Klerman, G. "Differentiating Depressed from Anxious Neurotic Outpatients." *Archives of General Psychiatry,* 1974, *30,* 302-308.
Rainey, J. M., Pohl, R. B., Williams, M., and others. "A Comparison of Lactate and Isoproterenol Anxiety States." *Psychopathology,* 1984, *17* (suppl. 1), 74-82.
Roberts, A. H. "Housebound Housewives—A Follow-up Study of a Phobic Anxiety State." *British Journal of Psychiatry,* 1964, *110,* 191-197.
Robins, L. N., Helzer, J. E., Croughan, J., and others. "National Institute of Mental Health Diagnostic Interview Schedule." *Archives of General Psychiatry,* 1981, *38,* 381-389.
Robins, L. N., Helzer, J. E., Weissman, M. M., and others. "Lifetime Prevalence of Psychiatric Disorders at Three Sites." *Archives of General Psychiatry,* 1984, *41,* 949-959.
Roth, M., Gurney, C., Garside, R. F., and others. "Studies in the Classification of Affective Disorders." *British Journal of Psychiatry,* 1972, *121,* 147-161.
Schapira, K., Roth, M., Kerr, T. A., and others. "The Prognosis of Affective Disorders: The Differentiation of Anxiety States from Depressive Illnesses." *British Journal of Psychiatry,* 1972, *121,* 175-181.
Sheehan, D. V., Sheehan, K. E., and Minichiello, W. E. "Age of Onset of Phobic Disorders: A Reevaluation." *Comprehensive Psychiatry,* 1981, *22,* 544-553.
Slater, E., and Shields, J., "Genetic Aspects of Anxiety." In M. H. Lader (ed.), *Studies of Anxiety.* London: Hedley Bros., 1969, 62-71.
Smail, P. "Alcohol Dependence and Phobic Anxiety States. I: A Prevalence Study." *British Journal of Psychiatry,* 1984, *144,* 53-57.
Spitzer, R. L., and Williams, J.B.W. "Revising DSM-III: The Process and Major Issues." Paper presented at DSM-III: An Interim Appraisal, sponsored by the

Committee to Evaluate DSM-III, October 13-15, 1983.
Thyer, B. A., Parrish, R. T., Curtis, G. C., and others. "Age of Onset of DSM-III Anxiety Disorders." *Comprehensive Psychiatry,* 1985, *26,* 113-122.
Torgersen, S. "Genetics of Neuroses: The Effect of Sampling Variation upon the Twin Concordance Ratio." *British Journal of Psychiatry,* 1983, *142,* 126-132.
Tyrer, P., Casey, P., and Gall, J. "Relationship Between Neurosis and Personality Disorder." *British Journal of Psychiatry,* 1983, *142,* 404-408.
Uhlenhuth, E. H., Balter, M. B., Mellinger, G. D., and others. "Symptom Checklist Syndromes in the General Population." *Archives of General Psychiatry,* 1983, *40,* 1167-1173.
Van Valkenburg, C., Akiskal, H. S., Puzantian, V., and others. "Anxious Depressions." *Journal of Affective Disorders,* 1984, *6,* 67-82.
Weissman, M. M., Lechman, J. F., Merikangas, K. R., and others. "Depression and Anxiety Disorders in Parents and Children." *Archives of General Psychiatry,* 1984, *41,* 845-853.
Weissman, M. M., Myers, J. K., and Harding, P. S. "Psychiatric Disorders in a U.S. Urban Community: 1975-1976." *American Journal of Psychiatry,* 1978, *135,* 459-462.
Weissman, M. M., Tischler, G. L., Holzer, C. E., and others. "Six-Month Prevalence of Psychiatric Disorders in Three Communities." *Archives of General Psychiatry,* 1984, *41,* 959-971.
Wheeler, E. O., White, P. D., and Reed, E. W. "Neurocirculatory Asthenia (Anxiety Neurosis, Effort Syndrome, Neurasthenic)." *Journal of the American Medical Association,* 1950, *142,* 878-889.
Winokur, G., and Holemon. "Chronic Anxiety Neurosis: Clinical and Sexual Aspects." *Acta Psychiatrica Scandinavia,* 1963, *39,* 384-412.
Wolpe, J. "The Dichotomy Between Classical Conditioning and Cognitively Learned Anxiety." *Journal of Behavior Therapy and Experimental Psychiatry,* 1981, *12,* 35-42.
Woodruff, R. A., Guze, S. B., and Clayton, P. J. "Anxiety Neurosis Among Psychiatric Outpatients." *Comprehensive Psychiatry,* 1972, *13,* 165-170.

James Reich is assistant professor of psychiatry at the University of Iowa College of Medicine.

Several disorders are encompassed in the clinical spectrum of anxiety. They are presented here according to current classification.

Identifying Panic Disorders

Eduardo Barreto, Henry Amado

This chapter details clinical presentation, laboratory tests, differential diagnosis, follow-up studies, family studies, and treatment trials to provide a framework for the identification of panic disorder.

Clinical Picture/Presentation

We refer here only to "endogenous" panic disorders; those involving unprovoked anxiety attacks in which the subjective experience of fear is accompanied by cardiorespiratory symptoms. This definition precludes anxiety attacks related to external stimuli, including phobias, stress disorders, and obsessive-compulsive disorders.

The DSM-III (APA, 1980) diagnostic criteria are as follows:

1. At least three panic attacks within a three-week period in circumstances other than during marked physical exertion or in a life-threatening situation. The attacks are not precipitated only by exposure to a circumscribed phobic stimulus.

2. Panic attacks are manifested by discrete periods of apprehension or fear. At least four of the following symptoms appear during each attack:

- Dyspnea
- Palpitations
- Chest pain or discomfort

R. A. Muñoz (ed.). *Treating Anxiety Disorders.*
New Directions for Mental Health Services, no. 32. San Francisco: Jossey-Bass, Winter 1986.

- Choking or smothering sensations
- Dizziness, vertigo, or unsteady feelings
- Feelings of unreality
- Paresthesias (tingling in hands or feet)
- Hot and cold flashes
- Sweating
- Faintness
- Trembling or shaking
- Fear of dying, going crazy, or doing something uncontrolled during an attack.

3. Not due to a physical disorder or another mental disorder, such as major depression, somatization disorder, or schizophrenia.
4. The disorder is not associated with agoraphobia.

Natural History

Although some patients develop varying degrees of nervousness and apprehension between attacks (Pasnau and others, 1984), panic lasting many hours or days probably represents residual anxiety or a condition other than panic disorder. The attacks usually begin suddenly and last for minutes, rarely for hours. The absence of any precipitant, the sudden emergence of symptoms without warning, differentiates this disorder from an otherwise normal anxiety response to threat.

The frequency of panic attacks varies among patients. Some experience them on a daily basis, while others develop them only once or twice a year. The age of onset is usually in the twenties and seldom after age 35 (Goodwin and Guze, 1984).

Patients with panic disorder often vividly recall the first attack. Typically that first attack occurs unexpectedly and suddenly while the patient is engaged in some innocuous activity. The patients may believe they are dying of a heart attack or losing their mind. The first attack may also begin insiduously, preceded by feelings of tension, nervousness, fatigue, or dizziness for years (Goodwin and Guze, 1984).

After the first panic attack, anxiety often returns to a normal level, and each subsequent panic attack tends to include the same cluster of symptoms for a particular patient. During every attack the patient may again seek emergency medical consultation, may be assured that no medical problems exist, and may receive benzodiazepines.

Most patients develop some degree of anticipatory anxiety, generated by the fear of having another panic attack, so that with each successive attack the level of anticipatory anxiety increases. Under these circumstances, a mistaken diagnosis of generalized anxiety disorder can be made (Gorman and others, 1984).

The patients are at first apt to interpret their symptoms as manifestations of medical illnesses, select one symptom from a large array, and seek out a specialist for that problem; for example, they commonly present with cardiorespiratory symptoms and may consult a cardiologist. Patients with panic disorder are often referred by cardiologists to psychiatrists after extensive evaluations. The patients sometimes are reluctant to see a psychiatrist because they perceive their disorder as "a heart condition," "something wrong with my chest," or a similar problem.

Patient A. Mr. A was a forty-five-year-old priest whose father had died from a heart attack and whose paternal uncle was being treated for coronary heart disease. He reported a twenty-five-year history of intermittent fear accompanied by shortness of breath, palpitations, chest pain, choking, and a feeling of impending doom. His relatives always thought he had a "weak heart" and was predisposed to a lethal heart attack. Mr. A was not satisfied when his cardiologist insisted that he had no heart condition and his symptoms were suggestive of a panic disorder.

During the first psychiatric interview, his description of his life suggested that it was unlikely that he had had any conflicts leading to a psychiatric disorder. He could not appreciate that the disorder might exist without deep intrapsychic conflict, and he was not certain that he would accept psychiatric care even if the only clear diagnosis were one of panic disorder.

Mr. A had led a very sheltered life. Whenever possible he had avoided responsibility, had opted for assignments that required limited interaction with others, and had accepted jobs in which he was an assistant rather than a principal actor.

Laboratory Tests

Many medical conditions present with the signs and symptoms of acute panic attacks, so that careful evaluation is mandatory to establish a differential diagnosis. Dietch (1981) reports that the diagnosis of panic disorder may be facilitated by a short hospitalization to obtain diagnostic studies and to observe the patient's symptoms. Laboratory tests that might be helpful during an acute episode include EKG; arterial blood gases; blood glucose; serum; calcium; T3, T4, T3 uptake; and a urine metanephrine assay.

There is no specific laboratory test for the diagnosis of panic disorder, but there are some controversial tests that are still under research:

1. Sodium lactate infusion appears to provoke panic attacks in about 80 percent of patients with panic disorder but not produce panic in normal controls (Leibowitz and others, 1984, Sheehan and others, 1985) or in patients with depression (Pitts and McClure, 1967).

2. Positron emission tomography may detect abnormalities of cerebral blood flow (left hemisphere less than right) in the parahippocampal gyri of patients with panic disorder (Reiman and others, 1984).

3. Evaluation of levels of neurotransmitters and their response to provocative agents (Gorman and others, 1984, Carr and Sheehan, 1984) may also add to full evaluation, but its value is yet uncertain.

4. A peptide, DBI (Diazepam Binding Inhibitor), in human and rat brains binds to the same receptor through which benzodiazepines exert their effect. This peptide, which increases anxiety, is located in the hypothalamus and medial amygdaloid nucleus. It may serve as a source of one or more smaller peptides that bind to the receptor. Attempts to determine the amino acid sequence and clone the gene are still in progress (Marx, 1984). The identification of the peptide may provide a better understanding of the intracerebral events that could be related to panic attacks, and thereby perhaps provide a sound therapeutic rationale for the use of anxiolytics.

Patient B. *Washington University Magazine* (Hagan, 1985) refers to the history of Mr. B, who took his final exam in history one spring day in 1974. He remembers, "I was writing away when all of a sudden, for no apparent reason, my heart started to race. I could hardly breathe. I got to feeling very fearful, and I got scared, really scared. I thought I was having a heart attack, so when I came out, a friend took me to the hospital near campus. They gave me a physical and told me there was nothing wrong, that I was not having a heart attack. I left for home still wondering what had happened."

After a long quest that included evaluations by several therapists, Mr. B finally received the diagnosis of the panic disorder. As part of the studies leading to his diagnosis, Mr. B received an infusion of lactate solution that, as is common in patients with panic disorders, reproduced all his symptoms. Before the infusion of lactate, it was considered that Mr. B had no history of significant medical illnesses, and a complete physical examination with measurement of vital signs to rule out any physical disease that might contraindicate lactate infusion was performed. Further work-up included normal electrolytes, glucose, BUN, liver function, CBC, urinalysis, and EKG (Sheehan and others, 1985). During the procedure, the patient was observed at least six hours before the infusion began. The dose of sodium lactate used was 10 cc/kg body weight infused over twenty minutes (Sheehan and others, 1985).

Mr. B and other patients participated in studies in which measurements of blood flow were taken on both sides of the brain in seven areas suspected of mediating anxiety. Only one of these areas—the parahippocampal gyrus—displayed an imbalanced blood flow in all patients who had a history of panic disorder and developed symptoms when they were infused with lactate.

Differential Diagnosis

"Organic Anxiety"

Some medical conditions must be considered before the diagnosis of panic disorder can be made. They include cardiopulmonary disorders, endocrine disorders, neurologic disorders, and toxic/metabolic states (Dietch, 1981).

Cardiopulmonary Disorders. *Angina pectoris* is confused with panic attacks mainly when the patient experiences chest discomfort rather than pain, or when the precipitant factors are atypical (Dietch, 1981). It has been pointed out (Banks and Shugoll, 1967) that the distinction between chest pain caused by coronary artery disease and that attributed to noncardiac factors is often very difficult. Among patients who have chest pains and normal coronary arteries, approximately two thirds have psychiatric rather than cardiac disorders (Goodwin and Guze, 1984). The symptoms in these patients are likely to represent the somatic manifestations of anxiety and not the consequences of heart disease. In one study of patients who had received the diagnosis of angina pectoris, postmortem examinations failed to show coronary artery narrowing in almost half the cases (Leibow and Oseasohn, 1964).

Patients with *cardiac arrhythmias* present commonly with symptoms of anxiety or acute panic attacks (Dietch, 1981).

Hyperkinetic heart syndrome, also known as *hyperdynamic beta adrenergic circulatory state,* presents with acute or chronic symptoms. The complaints of palpitations or simply increased cardiac awareness are prominent. *Recurrent pulmonary emboli* may present with repeated episodes of acute anxiety associated with marked hyperventilation and dyspnea (Ferrer, 1968).

Endocrine Disorders. Both *hyperthyroidism* and *hypothyroidism* may present in the early clinical stages as pure panic attacks, and the symptom distinction from panic disorder can be very difficult (Bowen, 1983).

Pheochromocytoma is a rare benign medullary tumor whose symptoms might be difficult to differentiate from those of an acute panic attack. Patients who have arterial hypertension, or patients who fail to respond to usual management of panic disorder or have predominant symptoms of warmth and flushing, are candidates for a pheochromocytoma work-up.

Hypoglycemia may be a manifestation of at least twenty distinct rare disorders (Arky and others, 1979) and may mimic the autonomic symptoms of panic disorder.

Hypoparathyroidism may present with anxiety as the primary symptom. This is true for the 20 percent of patients with this disorder that present with psychiatric features (Dietch, 1981).

In *Cushing's syndrome* anxiety occurs often but it is usually associated with other psychiatric manifestations, primarily depression or psychosis.

Neurologic Disorders. Partial complex seizures present with a variety of episodic symptoms that can simulate panic disorders. A common aura to seizures is a feeling of fear, fright, or dread (Daly, 1975).

Toxic/Metabolic Disorders. Medications that may trigger panic attacks may include thyroid preparations, cold pills, ephedrine, aminophylline, amphetamines, methylphenidate, phenmetrazine, levodopa, antihistamines, and indomethacin (Dietch, 1981).

Substances also include nicotine, caffeine, and cocaine. Withdrawal from opiate, barbiturates, sedative-hypnotics, nicotine, alcohol, and tricyclic antidepressants may also trigger attacks (Gawin and Markoff, 1981).

Other Disorders. There is a group of patients who have *hyperventilation syndrome* (HVS) but do not have the criteria for panic disorder. It is not known whether HVS is a symptomatic of other psychiatric or medical conditions or is a discrete syndrome (Goodwin and Guze, 1984).

A large number of other organic conditions have been known to present with anxiety, associated to more prominent signs and symptoms. Included are Wilson's disease, acute intermittent porphyria, SLE, chronic pulmonary disease, aortic arch syndrome, intracranial tumors, menopause, neuroleptic-induced akathisia, and tyramine-induced crisis in patients taking a monoamine oxidase inhibitor (Dietch, 1981).

Other Psychiatric Conditions

The psychiatric differential diagnosis of panic disorder is very challenging because anxiety symptoms and panic attacks can be part of almost any psychiatric illness. Many patients with panic disorder report a complex of symptoms, including phobias, excessive preoccupation with their health (hyponchondriasis), and multiple "hysterical" symptoms (Sheehan and others, 1983).

Panic attacks occur in any of several "primary" disorders, divided by DSM-III into four categories:

1. Phobic Disorders: If the patient presents with panic attacks and agoraphobia, the diagnosis will be agoraphobia with panic attack, and not panic disorder. Phobic disorders are ruled in when phobias are the predominant symptom, and ruled out when the patient is not certain what situations provoke the attacks.

There is no reliable way to predict which patient will develop agoraphobia or limited phobic avoidance. In a longitudinal study of 38 patients with panic disorder, Uhde and others (1985) found moderate to extreme agoraphobia and moderate to severe generalized anxiety in 84 percent.

The diagnosis of social phobia can be difficult since most patients with agoraphobia will also say that there are social situations that they are afraid to enter. The differentiation from phobia is based in the history that in patients with panic disorders the fear is of embarrassment for having a panic attack in such a situation. The individual with social phobia is afraid of an experience that only happens in a social situation, such as choking on food eaten in the presence of other people. There are some nebulous areas, such as when patients with typical panic attacks develop secondary situational phobias.

2. Anxiety States: Generalized anxiety disorder (GAD) includes patients who have had chronic anxiety for at least one month. A history of recurrent unprovoked panic attacks precludes the diagnosis of GAD. Anderson and others (1984) compared panic disorder with generalized anxiety disorder and found that patients with GAD have fewer autonomic symptoms, an earlier, more gradual onset, a more chronic course, and a more favorable outcome. The differentiation between generalized anxiety disorder and the anticipatory anxiety seen in panic attacks might be very difficult (Gorman and others, 1984).

The distinction can be seen on the basis of several facts:

- Medications that are effective with panic disorders are not useful in generalized anxiety disorder.
- Patients with panic disorder develop panic attacks during sodium lactate infusions, while patients with generalized anxiety disorder do not (Leibowitz and others, 1984).
- Panic disorder has a unique genetic basis (Crowe and others, 1983).
- Panic disorder, unlike generalized anxiety disorder in many cases, leads to specific types of phobic avoidance.

3. Post-Traumatic Stress Disorder: Post-traumatic stress disorder (PTSD) may present with panic attacks. Other manifestations of PTSD permit the differential diagnosis. In panic disorder the cardiopulmonary symptoms usually occur only in the context of panic attacks. This makes the differentiation from somatization disorders. However, somatization disorder may coexist with panic disorder, in which case both diagnoses should be made.

4. Atypical Anxiety Disorder: Panic disorder is an illness frequently complicated by either secondary affective disorder or alcoholism. Fifty percent of patients with panic disorder seen in a psychiatric clinic (Woodruff and others, 1972) gave a history of secondary depression. Uhde and associates (1985) found that 50 percent of patients with panic disorder had a lifetime history of depression, but only 24 percent had ever had depressive episodes that met DSM-III criteria for the diagnosis of major depression. Coryell and others (1982) followed a group of formerly hospitalized panic disorder patients and found unexpectedly high rates of suicide and cardiovascular disease. Secondary depression and alcoholism may have had a role.

Some patients probably abuse alcohol in attempts to self-medicate (Quitkin and Rabkin, 1982). Alcohol has a temporary ameliorative effect on anticipatory anxiety. Many alcoholics have a history of anxiety preceding the alcoholism.

Patient C. We have followed Mr. C for longer than ten years. His history has been well documented in records from a number of veterans' hospitals and community hospitals in four different states. In Mr. C's family there have been successful bankers, lawyers, and physicians, several of whom have had the diagnosis of bipolar affective disorder. Mr. C completed college at the age of twenty years and entered the army, graduating as a lieutenant. During World War II, he undertook training as a pilot, but his severe and repeated panic attacks led him to quit training and to join the infantry, where, as a captain, he won several medals and commendations for valor. He left the army and became a successful businessman. He then suffered occasional panic attacks, which he could not attribute to environmental circumstances. At age twenty-nine he suffered the first of a number of severe episodes of depression, which have continued to occur every four or five years up to now (he is sixty-five years of age). After the first episode of depression, Mr. C started drinking heavily and soon developed various complications of alcoholism, including benders, blackouts, inability to control his drinking, tremulousness, convulsions, and DT's. When we first evaluated him, the most obvious problem was alcoholism, but the history and the medical records permitted the diagnosis of major depressive disorder and panic disorder, with the latter being the first disorder to present chronologically.

In DSM-III a diagnosis of affective disorder preempts a diagnosis of panic disorder. Most likely in DSM-IIIR a patient who fulfills the criteria for major depressive episode and for panic disorder will have a joint diagnosis of panic disorder and major depressive episode (Pasnau and others, 1984).

Panic attacks do not justify being listed as a second diagnosis when the primary diagnosis is schizophrenia or major depression. The distinction between depressive disorders and panic disorder is based on chronology. Secondary panic disorder is diagnosed in the presence of the following:

- A present or pre-existing major depression; or
- A life-threatening or incapacitating medical illness that precedes and parallels the symptoms of panic disorder.

There has been speculation that panic disorder is a variation of affective disorder. Similarities between acute episodes of anxiety and depression have been observed (Klein and Fink, 1962). In Uhde and others (1985) longitudinal study, panic disorder was commonly associated with depressive symptomatology, although only 24 percent of patients developed longstanding endogenous symptoms. Generic studies indicate that there is an overlap of depression and panic disorder in the relatives of depressed patients (Lechman and others, 1983; Cadoret, 1978).

Arguments against the illnesses being identical are as follows:

1. The suicide rate of patients with major depression is much greater than that of patients with panic disorder.
2. Panic attacks can usually be precipitated in patients with panic disorder by the intravenous infusion of sodium lactate, while this rarely happens in depressed controls (Pitts and McClure, 1967).

3. Panic disorder has an earlier age-onset than primary affective disorder.
4. The efficacy of antidepressants in panic disorder may not be related to the concomitant presence of depressive symptomatology (Nurnberg and Coccaro, 1982; Zitrin and others, 1983; Klein, 1983).
5. Panic disorder patients do not exhibit the severity of depressive symptomatology seen in patients with major depressive disorders.
6. In follow-up studies there is very little crossover between panic disorder and depressive disorder (Schapira and others, 1972).

The phenomenological relationship among symptoms of depression and panic attacks remains controversial, and additional studies are indicated to elucidate the relationship of these symptoms.

Family History

Panic disorder, as mentioned by Goodwin and Guze (1984, p. 78), is "a familial condition with a lifetime morbidity risk between 18 percent and 22 percent among first-degree relatives." This is about twice what is expected in the general population and would indicate that once a case of anxiety neurosis is found, more are likely to be discovered in the same family. Recently, Crowe and others (1983) interviewed the relatives of patients diagnosed as having panic disorder or generalized anxiety disorder. The relatives had a lifetime morbidity risk of 24.7 percent for panic disorder, while relatives of controls had a risk of only 2.3 percent.

Monozygotic (MZ) twins have been found to be more concordant for panic disorders than dizygotic (DZ) twins. Slater and Shields (1969) found a higher concordance rate between MZ twins than between DZ twins. More recently, Torgersen (1983) examined 32 MZ and 53 DZ twins and found panic disorders five times more frequent in MZ than in DZ twins. In one family in which several members had panic disorders, two members had identical sibling pairs with panic disorders. They had similarly satisfactory therapeutic response to similar doses of tricyclic antidepressant (Surman and others, 1983).

Patient D. Miss D was a twenty-four-year-old probation officer who presented with typical anxiety attacks. We had an opportunity to interview her mother, two sisters, and a brother. They all had a lifelong history of "nervousness," and they also had had panic attacks of varying severity and frequency. The mother was a sixty-four-year-old housewife who had been described by the children as nervous and highstrung. She described repeated panic attacks thoughout her adult life, but never thought of obtaining treatment for them. The patient's two sisters had also had panic attacks, but much less frequently than the patient or their mother. They were aware of the problems their mother had had and tended not to give importance to their own symptoms. The brother, a twenty-seven-year-old police officer, remembered having panic attacks and much nervousness as he was growing up but also indicated that he had been asymptomatic for about five years.

Clinical Course and Complications

Without effective treatment the course of panic disorder is highly variable. Period of spontaneous remission occur intermittently and may last for months or even years. Wheeler and others (1950) published the first long-term study of a large population suffering panic disorder. After following 173 patients for twenty years, they concluded that panic disorder is usually a chronic condition that does not interfere significantly with the patient's work or social or family life and does not cause death. Twelve percent of their patients recovered, 35 percent had symptoms but no disability, and 15 percent had symptoms and moderate or severe disability. Panic attack patients do not have a high frequency of other diseases, do not suffer an unusual number of deaths, and seem to fare reasonably well in their social adjustment. These findings have been corroborated in several large studies (Goodwin and Guze, 1984; Marks and Caden, 1973).

Patient E. Mr. E, our oldest panic disorder patient, came to us at a senior citizen's clinic. At the age of eighty-four, he was a retired dentist who was distressed about his relationship with his seventy-two-year-old girlfriend. When we obtained a history, we learned that he had suffered anxiety attacks from the time he was in high school. He continued to suffer them during his period of service in World War I, when his attacks were attributed to possible gas poisoning. Subsequently, in dental school, he had fewer attacks, but they continued to be present throughout most of his successful practice as a dentist for close to fifty years. He was married twice and had three children. He was examined several times by different physicians, who suspected coronary heart disease. Subsequent studies failed to indicate any specific heart condition.

Treatment and Diagnosis

Patients with panic disorder, as opposed to those with generalized anxiety disorder, respond to treatment with tricyclic antidepressants or MAO inhibitors (Gorman and others, 1984). Using TCA or MAOI for blocking lactate-induced panic permits the identification of treatment-responsive patients.

Will there be a time when treatment can be used to corroborate a diagnosis? Should this happen, panic disorders could probably be among the psychiatric problems to show specificity of response to verbal therapy or pharmacologic interventions. Knowledge in this area is gradually increasing, and current information, though still tentative, permits one to visualize what the future may bring.

As an example, we will refer to a treatment scheme proposed by Sheehan (1983, p. 111–169). In his strategy the first target is biological, the second is the phobic component, and the third comprises the stresses that may accompany the disorder. We have already stated that in "pure" panic disorders phobias are by definition not a major problem, though secondary phobic behavior may be present in some patients.

Following Sheehan, we would first give medication such as alprazolam to outpatients with panic disorder. Alprazolam appears to be safer and faster than tricyclics and MAO inhibitors. Many patients may require nothing more. A phobic component may suggest behavior therapy. Any remaining difficulty could be corrected by addressing the patient's reaction to stress. Sheehan speaks of an eighteen-year-old patient by the name of Tammy. Correctly treated with medication and behavior therapy, she was not getting better. Her physician re-evaluated her condition and discovered that Tammy was afraid that should she recover, her grandfather would die. The therapist uncovered a complex situation in which the grandfather was dying, Tammy wanted to see him, and the father objected to that on account of her illness. Once the problem was clarified and Tammy visited the grandfather, the therapist was able to prepare the ways to a recovery.

Future Research and Controversial Issues

Diagnosis

1. The DSM-III (APA, 1980) has well-defined diagnostic criteria for organic affective, organic delusional, and organic personality syndromes and should contain a section on "organic anxiety disorders" (Bowen, 1983).

2. Interest in the mitral valve prolapse syndrome (MVPS) has increased in psychiatry with several studies reporting approximately 32 to 50 percent of patients with panic disorder also have MVPS (Hartman and others, 1982; Gorman and Fyer, 1981); this is higher than the natural prevalence of the condition. Other studies, however, reported a prevalence of MVPS in patients with panic disorder similar to that reported in normals. A family study of 50 patients with MVPS showed that panic attacks and MVPS segregate independently, a finding that would not be expected if MVPS caused the panic attack (Crowe and others, 1983).

3. Spitzer and Williams (1984) believe there is now sufficient clinical evidence to indicate that agoraphobia with panic attacks in most cases originates as panic disorder. In a proposed revision of the DSM-III such patients will be diagnosed as having panic disorder with extensive phobic avoidance (Pasnau and others, 1984).

4. There are questions about the diagnostic validity of generalized

anxiety disorder. It is suggested that it may be a prodromal, incomplete, or residual manifestation of other psychiatric disorders (Breier and Charney, 1985).

Conclusions

All patients with suspected diagnosis of panic disorder should have a medical history, a physical examination, and if necessary, laboratory tests to rule out "Organic Anxiety Syndrome" (Bowen, 1983). Circumstances in which the clinician should suspect an organic etiology include the following:

- If the patient's age of onset is greater than 35
- If there is no family history of anxiety disorder
- If the history or symptoms suggest a specific organic etiology
- If the subjective feelings of anxiety are unusual
- If there are unexplained laboratory or physical findings (Bowen, 1983).

The psychiatric work-up should evaluate these categories:

- Family history
- Age of onset
- Course of the disorder
- Appropriate physical and laboratory studies
- Response to treatment
- Typical symptoms of panic disorder
- Symptoms that differentiate panic disorder from other disorders (Bowen, 1983).

Further refinement of drug treatments, behavior interventions, and cognitive-interpersonal therapy may permit the use of rational, specific therapeutic interventions.

References

American Psychiatric Association. *Diagnostic and Statistical Manual of Mental Disorders.* (3rd ed.) Washington, D.C.: American Psychiatric Association, 1980.

Anderson, D. J., Noyes, R., and Crowe, R. R. "A Comparison of Panic Disorder and Generalized Anxiety Disorder." *American Journal of Psychiatry,* 1984, *141,* 572–575.

Arky, R. A., Inde Groot, G. J., Cahill, G. F., and Martini, R. *Hypoglycemia: Endocrinology.* Vol. 2. New York: Grunes and Stratton, 1979.

Banks, T., and Shugoll, G. I. "Confirmatory Physical Findings in Angina Pectoris." *Journal of the American Medical Association,* 1967, *200,* 1031–1035.

Bowen, R. C. "Differential Diagnosis of Anxiety Disorders." *Progress in Neurology, Psychopharmacology, and Biological Psychiatry,* 1983, *7,* 605–609.

Breier, A., and Charney, D. S. "The Diagnostic Validity of Anxiety Disorders and Their Relationship to Depressive Illness." *American Journal of Psychiatry,* 1985, *142,* 787–797.

Cadoret, R. "Genetic Principles in the Taxonomy of Affective Disorder." In J. Aliskal and W. Webb (eds.), *Psychiatric Diagnosis.* New York: Spectrum, 1978.

Carr, D., and Sheehan, D. V. "Panic Anxiety: A New Biological Model." *Journal of Clinical Psychiatry,* 1984, *45,* 323-330.

Coryell, W., Noyes, R., and Clancy, J. "Excess Mortality in Panic Disorder: A Comparison with Primary Unipolar Depression." *Archives of General Psychiatry,* 1982, *39,* 701-703.

Crowe, R. R., Noyes, R., Pauls, D. L., and Slymen, D. "A Family Study of Panic Disorder." *Archives of General Psychiatry,* 1983, *40* (10), 1065-1069.

Daly, D. D. "Total Clinical Manifestations of Complex Partial Seizures." In J. K. Penny and D. D. Daly (eds.), *Complex Partial Seizures and Their Treatment.* New York: Raven Press, 1975.

Dietch, J. "Diagnosis of Organic Anxiety Disorders." *Psychosomatics,* 1981, *22* (8), 661-669.

Ferrer, M. "Mistaken Psychiatric Referral of Occult Serious Cardiovascular Disease." *Archives of General Psychiatry,* 1968, *18,* 112-113.

Gawin, R. M., and Markoff, R. A. "Panic Anxiety After Abrupt Discontinuation of Amitryptyline." *American Journal of Psychiatry,* 1981, *138,* 117-118.

Goodwin, D. W., and Guze, S. B. *Psychiatric Diagnosis.* (3rd ed.) New York: Oxford University Press, 1984.

Gorman, J. M., and Fyer, A. J. "Mitral Valve Prolapse and Panic Disorder: Effect of Imipramine." In D. F. Klein and J. H. Rabkin (eds.), *Anxiety: New Research and Changing Concepts.* New York: Raven Press, 1981.

Gorman, J. M., Leibowitz, M. R., and Klein, D. F. *Panic Disorder and Agoraphobia: Current Concepts.* Kalamazoo, Mich.: The Upjohn Company, 1984.

Hagan, S. "When Fear Strikes." *Washington University Magazine,* 1985, *55,* 12-15.

Hartman, N., Kramer, R., Brown, W. T., and Devereux, R. B. "Panic Disorder in Patients with Mitral Valve Prolapse." *American Journal of Psychiatry,* 1982, *139,* 669-679.

Klein, D. F. "Is the Antipanic Activity of Antidepressant Medications Reflective of Antidepressant Effect?" *Integrative Psychiatry,* 1983, *1,* 26-27.

Klein, D. F., and Fink, M. "Psychiatric Reaction Patterns to Imipramine." *American Journal of Psychiatry,* 1962, *119,* 432-438.

Lechman, J. F., Merikangas, K. R., Pauls, D., Prusoff, B. A., and Weissman, M. M. "Anxiety Disorders Associated with Episode of Depression: Family Study Data Contradict DSM-III Convention." *American Journal of Pychiatry,* 1983, *140,* 880-882.

Leibow, I. M., and Oseasohn, R. "Relationships Between Selected Clinical and Electrocardiographic Findings and Post Mortem Lesions Associated with Ischemic Heart Diseases." *Journal of Chronic Disorders,* 1964, *17,* 609-717.

Leibowitz, M. R., and others. "Lactate Provocation of Panic Attacks." *Archives of General Psychiatry,* 1984, *41.*

Marks, I., and Caden, M. "Anxiety States: A Review." *Journal of Nervous Mental Disorders,* 1973, *156,* 3-18.

Marx, J. L. " 'Anxiety Peptide' Found in Brain." *Science,* 1984, *227,* 934.

Nurnberg, G. H., and Coccaro, E. F. "Response of Panic Disorder and Resistance of Depression to Imipramine." *American Journal of Psychiatry,* 1982, *139,* 1060-1062.

Pasnau, R. O., Shader, R. L., Williams, J. B., Rubin, R. T., Shine, R. I., Klein, D. F., and Freedman, D. K. "Panic Disorders: Clinical Update." *Psychosomatics,* 1984, *25* (10), 1-30.

Pitts, F. N., and McClure, J. N. "Lactate Metabolism in Anxiety Neurosis." *New England Journal of Medicine,* 1967, 1329-1336.
Quitkin, F., and Rabkin, J. "Hidden Psychiatric Diagnosis in the Alcoholic." In *Alcoholism and Clinical Psychiatry.* New York: Plenum, 1982.
Reiman, F. M., Raichle, M. E., Butler, F. K., Herscovitch, P., and Robins, E. "A Focal Brain Abnormality in Panic Disorder: A Severe Form of Anxiety," *Nature,* 1984, *310* (23), 683-684.
Schapira, K., Roth, M., Kerr, T. A., and others. "The Prognosis of Affective Disorders: The Differentiation of Anxiety States from Depressive Illnesses." *British Journal of Psychiatry,* 1972, *121,* 175-181.
Sheehan, D. V. *The Anxiety Disease.* New York: Scribner's, 1983.
Sheehan, D. V., Carr, D. B., Fishman, S. M., Walsh, M. M., and Peltzier, D. S. "Lactate Infusion in Anxiety Research: Its Evolution and Practice." *Journal of Clinical Psychiatry,* 1985, *47,* 158-165.
Sheehan, D. V., Davidson, J., Manschrecks, and others. "Lack of Efficacy of a New Antidepressant (Bupropion) in the Treatment of Panic Disorder with Phobias." *Journal of Clinical Psychopharmacology,* 1983, *3,* 28-31.
Slater, E., and Shields, J. "Genetic Aspects of Anxiety." In M. H. Lader (ed.), *Studies of Anxiety.* London: Headley Bros., 1969.
Spitzer, R. L., and Williams, J.B.W. "Anxiety Disorders: Diagnostic Consideration in Psychiatry." In *Update.* Vol. 3, American Psychiatric Press, 1984.
Surman, O. S., Sheehan, D. V., Fuller, T. C., and Gallo, J. "Panic Disroder in Genotypic HLA Identical Sibling Pairs." *American Journal of Psychiatry,* 1983, *140,* 237-238.
Torgersen, S. "Genetic Factors in Anxiety Disorders." *Archives of General Psychiatry,* 1983, *40,* 1085-1089.
Uhde, T. E., Boulenger, J. P., Roy-Byrne, P. P., Geraw, M. F., Vittone, B. J., and Post, R. M. "Longitudinal Course of Panic Disorder: Clinical and Biological Consideration." *Progress in Neurology, Psychopharmacology, and Biological Psychiatry,* 1985, *9,* 39-51.
Wheeler, E. O., White, P. D., Reed, E. W., and Cohen, M. E. "Neurocirculatory Asthenia (Anxiety Neurosis, Effort Syndrome, Neuroasthenic)." *Journal of the American Medical Association,* 1950, *142,* 878-889.
Woodruff, R. A., Guze, S. B., and Clayton, P. J. "Anxiety Neurosis Among Psychiatric Outpatients." *Comprehensive Psychiatry,* 1972, *13,* 165-170.
Zitrin, L. M., Klein, D. F., Woerner, M. G., and Ross, P. C. "Treatment of Phobias: Comparison of Imipramine Hydrochloride and Placebo." *Archives of General Psychiatry,* 1983, *40,* 125-138.

Eduardo Barreto is a physician at Veteran's Administration Hospital in San Diego, California.

Henry Amado is clinical coordinator of the Western Mood and Sleep Disorders Institute in San Diego.

Cognitive behavioral interventions offer short-term methods to cope with anxiety. Focusing on personal perceptions, this approach expands nonmedical treatments for anxiety.

Cognitive Therapy for Anxiety Disorders

Wayne A. Bowers

Anxiety is viewed as part of life and for this reason has not been thought amenable to treatment (Beck and Emery, 1979). However, anxiety is reported as one of the most persistent problems confronting health care providers. Polls and research studies indicate that 30 to 40 percent of the population admit to symptoms of anxiety (Marsland, Wood, and Mayo, 1979), and anxiety is the fifth most commonly reported reason to visit a physician (Shepherd, Cooper, Brown, and Kalton, 1966).

Despite the rampant incidence of anxiety in the general public, this disorder has received less study than depression or schizophrenia. Even when research has focused on this disorder, the growth in treatment is at best uneven, addressing interventions for phobias and obsessive-compulsive disorders (Barlow and Beck, 1984) and, recently, agoraphobia (Barlow and Wolfe, 1981; Mathews, Gelder, and Johnston, 1981).

Treatments that exist fall into three primary categories—pharmacological, behavioral, and cognitive. The pharmacological interventions for anxiety use tricyclics (primarily imipramine) and MAO inhibitors (Barlow and Beck, 1984). These drugs target physiological symptoms that may have a direct effect on the cognitive/affective mechanisms. Other medications used to treat anxiety include minor tranquilizers (Valium, Librium) and, recently, propranolol (Wolpe, 1982). These drugs reduce or alleviate somatic symptoms that may herald anxiety.

R. A. Muñoz (ed.). *Treating Anxiety Disorders.*
New Directions for Mental Health Services, no. 32. San Francisco: Jossey-Bass, Winter 1986.

Behavioral interventions also focus on somatic symptoms of anxiety. Relaxation has been used to help individuals cope with anxiety (Borkovec and Sides, 1979). Progressive muscle relaxation (Jacobson, 1938) and its many variations reduce anxiety in many different disorders. However, relaxation is generally an adjunct procedure to other interventions, such as systematic desensitization or in vivo exposure (Marks, 1978). Biofeedback is another nonpharmacological intervention that reduces anxiety.

Two studies have revealed its reduction of anxiety in general anxiety disorders (Arnarson and Sheffield, 1980; Townsend, House, and Addario, 1975). Canter, Kondo, and Knott (1975) favor EMG feedback when working with anxiety disorders because there are no physical risks to the patient.

Behavioral approaches to anxiety have been utilized primarily when treating phobias and obsessive-compulsive disorders (Barlow and Beck, 1984; Leitenberg, 1976). Exposure in vivo either by flooding or by a graded form of intervention has shown positive results (Marks, 1981). Exposure through imagery is also used to help reduce anxiety.

More recently, cognitive methods are being used to grapple with anxiety problems. These methods borrow from behavior therapy but place a prominent role upon cognitions in the development of anxiety disorders. The cognitive theory and the interventions utilize the thought processing of the individual being treated.

Cognitive Theory of Anxiety

The genesis of anxiety is either physical (for example, an attack by a dog) or social (for example, a threat to self-esteem). In either case the precipitating event is distorted by the cognitive processing of the individual. Once the event has occurred, it can be generalized to other areas as long as there remains a threat to the individual.

The anxious individual imagines harmful situations and then projects himself or herself into them. Once in such a dreadful situation (real or imagined), the individual dwells on the outcome and underestimates his or her own ability to perform. The images created (cognitions) can become strong enough to induce the physiological symptoms of anxiety. As the attacks of anxiety persist, the individual dreads the unpleasant symptoms as strongly as the precipitating cause.

Cognitive/behavioral theory postulates a significant relationship among the cognitive, behavioral, and affective processes of an individual and that cognitions influence the intensity of the anxiety reaction. This theory states that the experience of fear is linked not only to the actual situation but also to images and symbols representing the past and the future. (For a more detailed discussion see Beck and Emery, 1979; Beck, Emery, and Greenberg, 1985.) Fear signals a threat to the individual, which calls for a response to protect one's well-being. Anxiety, on the other hand, is the emotional and physiological response that accompanies fear. Anxiety symptoms inhibit or interfere with successful coping strategies. When this inhibition occurs, the feedback mechanism that normally helps an individual cope becomes a serious threat. The anxious individual systematically distorts innocuous events, exaggerates the potential for harm, and perseverates on thought or visual images about being physically or psychologically harmed. Incoming data is shaped to fit the individual's idea of how his or her well-being will be affected. The individual's awareness and labeling of a noxious situation is followed by an assessment of what self-protective resources and coping mechanisms exist. The degree of anxiety is weighed against the perceived threat and the ability to cope with the threat. The assessment of the situation and the ability to cope may cause the individual to perceive the external stimulus as more dangerous than it would be were it not for the anxious feelings. This assessment created a vicious loop in which anxiety reinforces fear and, in turn, anxiety.

The cognitive/behavioral model places a heavy reliance on the thinking processes of the individual. A common factor in the continuance of anxiety is the cognitive set or schema of the anxious person. A cognitive set helps an individual orient to his or her environment and focus on specific situations within that environment. It allows for response patterns to specific stimuli rather than others. In short, it helps a person quickly respond to the environment by reducing and organizing incoming information about the world. A cognitive set is adaptive when it allows for the greatest amount of information to be analyzed in the shortest period of time. For the anxious individual these sets are hypervalent and block out important information about their world or do not allow for information processing that is accurate to the situation and that permits functional behavior. The hyperactivity keeps the individual in what Beck (Beck, Emery, and Greenberg, 1985) calls a "danger mode"—constantly scanning his or her world for potential threats.

With this set in place, the anxious individual sets up a feedback loop that encompasses cognitive, affective, and behavioral processes. Sensory inputs are processed and relayed to cognitive sets that lead to the enhancement or reduction of behavior. This feedback loop continues until the individual perceives the danger to himself or herself is gone.

Cognitive/Behavior Therapy

Cognitive/behavioral therapy (CBT) is based on the theory that an individual's affect and behavior are in part determined by the way he or she views the world in relation to himself or herself and to the person's experiences and future (Beck, Rush, Shaw, and Emery, 1979). It is a time-limited, active, and fairly structured intervention that alerts an individual to various misperceptions about his world in order to restructure them (Turk, Meichenbaum, and Genest, 1983). Stressful and potentially stressful events are interpreted in a negative fashion, which contributes to feelings such as hopelessness, guilt, low self-esteem, or anxiety. When these misperceptions occur, the individual is likely to act in accordance with these thoughts and feelings, which, in turn, reinforce negative self-regard.

CBT helps to identify, test, and correct maladaptive, distorted, and dysfunctional belief systems. Connections between cognitions, affect, and behavior and their interaction are the primary focus. The person is encouraged to be aware of these interactions, monitor their consequence, and understand the role that negative thoughts and images play in the maintenance of maladaptive behavior. Interventions focus primarily on the nature of cognitions, feelings, and their modification. In general, CBT uses environmental manipulation that represents informational feedback to provide an opportunity for the person to hypothesize, test, reappraise, and acquire new coping skills over dysfunctional cognitions, feelings, and behaviors.

During therapy, the individual is encouraged to develop new views of the problems. A common method of facilitating change is through a Socratic type of interaction. Skillful questioning by the therapist guides the patient to reformulate his or her view of the world. It is important to help differentiate problems and not to set up an adversarial situation between the patient and the therapist. As part of the overall treatment approach, the therapist responds to selective statements, gives homework, offers possible explanations to be tested, encourages the patient to reconstruct or reinterpret problems. Reframing of problems is enhanced by collection of evidence (situations, feelings, or behaviors). This increases self-exploration and awareness, allowing the therapist and patient to define the problem and formulate interventions.

Treatment Model

Cognitive/behavioral therapy is an educative model that incorporates a phenomenological framework. It bases its treatment approach on the use of everyday experiences. Three primary components of this approach are automatic thoughts, schemas, and assumptions.

Automatic thoughts are short, instantaneous, evaluative statements about the self. Used as coping mechanisms, automatic thoughts may be either positive or negative in nature and may compel the individual to a specific act or behavior. Because they are instantaneous, they are generally outside our awareness and an effort must be made to bring them into awareness.

Schemas or personal sets are collections of experiences in memory that have to do with the self. Schemas are a developmental concept; they are continually being expanded by our experience. Schemas develop early in life and function as coping mechanisms for dealing with the world. A schema may be a word, a situation, or an image that prepares us to deal with new events. These experiences may have a positive or negative quality. When schemas are not expanded to meet new and existing information they can contribute to feelings of hopelessness and anxiety.

Like schemas and automatic thoughts, assumptions are also coping mechanisms. An assumption is a basic attitude or rule for living. They appear in "if . . . then" format. These rules for living are ironclad; when they are violated, the individual views himself or herself as a failure or a loser.

Distortions of perceptions are common among all people, but they seem to be more prevalent among those individuals with an anxious or depressed mood. These pessimistic ideas contribute to anxiety and hopelessness and usually are illogical and unrealistic. Cognitive distortions (Beck and others, 1979) represent world views taken by the client as truth. The patient is usually unable to see them for what they are, that is dysfunctional coping mechanisms. It is important to remember that all people use cognitive distortions at some time. It is when they are used exclusively to cope with the world that they become dysfunctional coping mechanisms.

The goal of CBT is to assist the client to gain new coping skills or enhance existing ones. This is accomplished by increasing the individual's awareness of automatic thoughts and the silent assumptions that foster and sustain emotional turmoil. Also of major importance is identifying and challenging cognitive distortions and replacing them with functional or realistic alternatives to the personal world. Along with the development of new coping mechanisms is a need to sharpen the individual's social skills (Childress and Burns, 1981).

Interventions

A complete understanding of the interventions used with CBT is beyond the scope of this paper. The interested reader is encouraged to read Beck, Emery, and Greenberg (1985) or Meichenbaum (1977) for a comprehensive understanding of these methods.

The cognitive model is based on a collaborative empiricism. It uses the actual problems of the individual in the "here and now" and works to solve them. The relationship between the therapist and the patient is also collaborative, with equal responsibility for progress falling on both individuals. Patient and therapist are equal partners in developing skills to cope with a changing world.

When using this model, it is very important to choose topics that are easily attainable using examples from the client's own immediate experience. Use of specific behaviors helps reduce the amount of outside interference that can come from a wide-open approach to therapy.

Targets for change can be broken down into two basic types—behavioral and cognitive. These two categories account for the majority of interventions in CBT.

Behavioral. Behavioral assignments are designed to increase movement and get the patient actively involved in treatment. The inertia that is sometimes seen in anxious individuals increases the likelihood of self-defeating personal perceptions (automatic thoughts, cognitive distortions). The following are some of the behavioral assignments used.

Graded Task Assignments. This technique can be utilized both in the session and as homework. (Homework will be discussed later.) Its targets are passivity and overgeneralized beliefs of inadequacy and incompetence. Tasks that seem overwhelming are broken into smaller parts to allow for their accomplishment. The therapist begins with a sample assignment established during the interview. More complex and demanding activities are gradually added as homework. With each successive mastered experience, the patient can move from simple to complex tasks. The patient might optionally collect cognitions associated with the task to show how personal success is undercut.

Activity Schedule Making. This task is aimed at decreasing passivity and increasing spontaneity by alleviating the patient's tendency to ruminate on not being able to do anything. The therapist and patient collaborate to schedule hourly daily activities. Activities are evaluated on the basis of how much they improve the patient's coping ability rather than on their importance.

Mastery and Pleasure Therapy. The activities that are garnered in the Activity Schedule can be rated for how much mastery (M) and pleasure (P) was produced in each. This rating will enable the client to see how she or he misperceives success. This task also facilitates identification and correction of cognitive distortions (Beck, Rush, and Kovacs, 1976).

In Vivo Experiments. The use of real-life situations to increase confidence is important in overcoming anxiety. This aids in validating ideas and beliefs about anxiety. In this procedure, sometimes called in vivo desensitization, the individual confronts those things that are feared using a hierarchy or a graded task assignment. This is accomplished by shaping or approaching the feared stimulus on a gradual basis. Discomfort causes the person to move away from the situation and then soon move back into the feared environment. This type of procedure can be used with or without the therapist.

It is apparent that behavioral interventions provide a base for the cognitive interventions. The focal point of much of this therapy is allowing the individual to descern dysfunctional awareness and correct them.

Cognitive. Altering thoughts, feelings, and behavior is a complex task, as these three components are intricately interwoven. The therapist attempts to process with the patient successes and failures during treatment but also how the person is thinking and feeling in response to success and failure. The goal is to change cognitions, feelings, and behaviors as the person goes about his or her daily affairs. Action-oriented interventions such as changing the present environment, engaging in various therapeutic tasks, or learning relaxation skills are encouraged. Also, emphasis is placed on using the support networks that exist for the patient.

The cognitive model trains individuals in problem solving. This is accomplished by instructing the person to be aware of the self-evaluations made during stressful or uncomfortable situations. The continued monitoring of the self-statements and reframing of stressful or symptomatic situations as a problem to be solved rather than a threat expands the range of alternative coping skills. Self-monitoring also enhances treatment generalization by creating cues that initiate more adaptive coping mechanisms.

Cognitive Procedures

Collection of Automatic Thoughts. This can be accomplished by (a) assigning a time to write down uncomfortable thoughts, (b) collecting thoughts at the time of a change in feeling states, (c) collecting the environmental associations that trigger the feelings, and (d) collecting the thoughts during the interview itself. Early on the counselor may need to point out the unreasonableness of these thoughts so that the client may ultimately become aware of his or her own misconceptions.

One aid to the collection of automatic thoughts is the use of the Daily Record of Dysfunctional Thoughts (DRDT). This is a written, structured procedure that enhances the client's ability to identify and correct automatic thoughts. In this procedure the client writes down any shift in affect, describes the situation in which it occurred, and identifies the concurrent automatic thoughts. After each automatic thought has been identified, it is challenged for its accuracy. Often it is helpful to identify a cognitive distortion as well. Once the challenge is made, the client then attempts to find a functional or alternative reason for the feeling state.

Identifying Cognitive Distortions. As the patient collects automatic thoughts, patterns of cognitive distortions emerge. The patterns involve such things as being abandoned, feeling like a failure, or fear of dying. The client begins to assess each error in perception and attempts to find the flaw in his or her logic. In this way the client will become more aware of the patterns of distorted thinking.

Typical cognitive distortions may include the following:

Selective Abstraction. Focusing on a detail taken out of context, ignoring other salient features of the situation and conceptualizing the whole experience on the basis of this fragment.

Overgeneralization. A pattern of drawing a general rule or conclusion on the basis of one or more isolated incidents and applying the concept across the board to related and unrelated situations.

Dichotomous Thinking. The tendency to place all experiences in one of two opposite categories, such as flawless or defective, immaculate or filthy, saint or sinner. In describing himself, the patient selects the extreme negative categorization (Beck and others, 1979, p. 14).

Testing Cognitions. Once a pattern is recognized, it is imperative that the client learn how to test the validity of the perceptions. This process is the hallmark of CBT. Two approaches are (1) distinguishing ideas from facts, and (2) checking observations. When separating facts from ideas, the client must be informed that his or her thoughts are not equivalent to the real world. Attempts are made to assist the client to shift from a deductive approach to viewing the world to an inductive procedure. "The basic therapeutic doctrine is as follows: Simply because the individual thinks something does not necessarily make it true" (Beck and others, 1976, p. 24). The accuracy of a client's judgments can be checked by assessing the completeness of the initial environmental observations. The identification of cognitive distortions facilitates this part of the therapy.

Identifying underlying assumptions is critical to the coping ability of the client. The focus is to bring into awareness attitudes and assumptions that contribute to the individual's feelings. The awareness and alteration of these assumptions lead to a modification and restructuring of belief systems. The way an individual sets standards, assesses and modifies behavior, or explains the occurrences in life derives from these basic assumptions.

Use of Homework

Homework assignments are crucial to the success of CBT. These assignments involve daily recording of thoughts and behaviors, counteracting negative cognitions, reading informational material, and practicing new behavior such as assertiveness. Homework facilitates the client's ability to generalize improvement from the office to the rest of his or her life. It serves as a reality test for the client to achieve what has been talked about in the office. It provides data for therapy and focuses the work from the subjective to the objective (Beck and others, 1976). Homework also provides session-to-session reference points for the client. As an integral part of treatment it is important that the client understand that without the homework very little will be accomplished in treatment.

Beck, Rush, and Kovacs (1976) suggest that homework

1. Insures realistic self-counseling;
2. Increases the probability of more adaptive behaviors;
3. Reinforces self-change in three ways: (a) It increases desired skills in realistic thinking, (b) it decreases the frequency of emotional conflict, and (c) it increases the ability to control behavior;
4. Provides tools for handling future problems.

Failure to accomplish homework is a red flag warning of the need to examine the therapy process. Two reasons for failing to follow through with homework are (1) that the assignment is too difficult, or (2) the client is choosing not to follow through or sabotaging the process. The counselor must be aware of how much the client can realistically accomplish and gauge assignments accordingly. If the assignment is not too difficult, the counselor must use this information as part of the counseling session to help the client cope with the new experience or assess whether the failure to do the homework is part of an automatic thought. Whatever the reason, prompt intervention is necessary.

Case Example

B. W. was a thirty-seven-year-old male who worked as an educator. A self-referral, B. W.'s chief complaint was anxiety and panic attacks. B. W. was free of psychiatric symptoms until age thirty-five, when he began to experience heart palpitations and chest pain while attending a football game. His condition was thoroughly evaluated by his local physician and a cardiologist, who found no physical reasons for his problems. His symptoms were occasional panic characterized by chest pain, cold sweats, tachycardia, muscle tightness, throat tightness, and a feeling of dread. During these spells, B. W. felt the need to escape his situation, fearing he would lose control and embarrass himself or others. Although the feelings of panic were not frequent, they did restrict his involvement in large crowds such as attend football or basketball games.

Upon examination B. W. presented as a neatly dressed and confident individual. He was working on a Ph.D. degree and receiving excellent reports on his job. He had many friends and socialized freely. He was involved in several social and professional organizations and was respected within the community. He was active in athletics and ran approximately five miles per day. There was no history of psychiatric illness in his family, and he denied excessive use of alcohol, tea, or coffee. He was given a diagnosis of panic disorder with traits of agoraphobia. At the time of diagnosis B. W. was taking an anti-anxiety medication. Not wishing to continue this treatment, he was tapered from his medication during the course of therapy. He was referred to a psychologist for cognitive therapy.

The first few sessions focused on B. W.'s understanding of his problem and an attempt to target areas on which to work. It was noted early that B. W. was very concerned about being in control, with any indication that he was not in control implying weakness and ineffectiveness. He started keeping a daily schedule, tracking times and situations in which he felt anxious. A long-term goal of traveling to Florida on vacation was established as a reference point for progress in therapy. B. W. saw this trip as a symbol of his ability to be in control, as he was fearful that he might experience a panic attack that would totally incapacitate him.

Concurrent with the daily activity schedule, B. W. was instructed to take progressively longer trips by himself away from his home. Upon entering treatment he could accomplish trips outside of his home community only in the company of his wife. B. W. was also asked to keep track of his thoughts and feelings during these trips. This was accomplished by completing a Daily Record of Dysfunctional Thoughts, which brought into awareness negative cognitions surrounding travel.

When using the DRDT, B. W. became more aware that to safeguard his well-being he must be in control. Any break in that control precipitated doubts about his competence and fear that others would see him as less than a "man." As he became more aware of these assumptions, he replaced these thoughts with more objective and functional beliefs. At the same time, B. W. took a long trip (approximately two hundred miles) as an indication of his progress. He was able to complete this trip with minimal anxiety and felt that he was ready to take his trip to Florida. This trip was considered a success for B. W., as he was able to complete it without suffering a panic attack. His primary mode of dealing with feelings of anxiety while traveling was to restructure cognitions surrounding feelings of anxiety into realistic views of his performance. He was able to pick out physical cues that heralded anxiety and focus on ways to restructure them. One approach was to ask how he was evaluating himself and then look for the objective evidence that this evaluation was true.

Therapy continued to focus on his distorted perceptions of being out of control, with more consistent use of cognitive procedures. One of B. W.'s primary cognitive distortions was the use of generalization. By the middle of therapy B. W. was tapered off his medication. Although still feeling somewhat anxious, he was confident in his ability to combat his anxiety by using skills developed during treatment. Sessions were reduced to three, then two times per month, with a goal of traveling on his own to a major metropolitan area. This trip was accomplished in the later stages of treatment, and B. W. was still experiencing some feelings of discomfort but was able to control them via cognitive methods.

References

Arnarson, E. O., and Sheffield, G. "The Generalization of the Effects of EMG and Temperature Biofeedback Procedures in Patients Suffering from Anxiety States." In *Proceedings of the Biofeedback Society of America, Eleventh Annual Meeting.* Denver: Biofeedback Society of America, 1980.

Barlow, D. H., and Beck, G. J. "The Psychosocial Treatment of Anxiety Disorders: Current Status, Future Directions." In J.B.W. Williams and R. L. Spitzer (eds.), *Psychotherapy Research: Where Are We and Where Should We Go.* New York: Guilford, 1984.

Barlow, D. H., and Wolfe, B. E. "Behavioral Approaches to Anxiety Disorders: A Report on the NIMH-SUNY, Albany Research Conference." *Journal of Consulting and Clinical Psychology,* 1981, *49,* 488–494.

Beck, A. T., and Emery, G. *Cognitive Therapy of Anxiety and Phobic Disorders.* Philadelphia: Center for Cognitive Therapy, 1979.
Beck, A. T., Emery, G., and Greenberg, R. L. *Anxiety Disorders and Phobias: A Cognitive Perspective.* New York: Basic Books, 1985.
Beck, A. T., Rush, A. J., and Kovacs, M. *Individual Treatment Manual for Cognitive/Behavioral Psychotherapy of Depression.* Unpublished manuscript, University of Pennsylvania and University of Oklahoma, 1976.
Beck, A. T., Rush, A. J., Shaw, B. F., and Emery, G. *Cognitive Therapy of Depression.* New York: Guilford, 1979.
Borkovec, T. D., and Sides, J. K. "Critical Procedural Variables Related to the Physiological Effects of Progressive Relaxation." *Behavior Research and Therapy,* 1979, *17,* 119–126.
Canter, A., Kondo, C. Y., and Knott, J. R. "A Comparison of EMG Feedback and Progressive Muscle Relaxation Training in Anxiety Neurosis." *British Journal of Psychiatry,* 1975, *127,* 470–477.
Childress, A. R., and Burns, D. D. "The Basics of Cognitive Therapy." *Psychosomatics,* 1981, *22* (12), 1017–1028.
Jacobson, E. *Progressive Relaxation.* Chicago: University of Chicago Press, 1938.
Leitenberg, H. *Handbook of Behavior Modification and Behavior Therapy.* Englewood Cliffs, N.J.: Prentice-Hall, 1976.
Marks, I. "Behavioral Psychotherapy of Adult Neurosis." In S. Garfield and A. Bergin (eds.), *Handbook of Psychotherapy and Behavior Change: An Empirical Analysis.* (2nd ed.) New York: Wiley, 1978.
Marks, I. M. *Cure and Care of Neurosis.* New York: Wiley, 1981.
Marsland, D. W., Wood, M., and Mayo, F. "Content of Family Practice: A Data Bank for Patient Care, Curriculum, and Research in Family Practice—526,196 Patient Problems." *Journal of Family Practice,* 1979, *3,* 25–68.
Mathews, A. M., Gelder, M. G., and Johnston, D. W. *Agoraphobia: Nature and Treatment.* New York: Guilford, 1981.
Meichenbaum, D. H. *Cognitive Behavior Modification: An Integrated Approach.* New York: Plenum, 1977.
Shepherd, M., Cooper, B., Brown, A. C., and Kalton, G. W. *Psychiatric Illness in General Practice.* London: Oxford University Press, 1966.
Townsend, R. E., House, J. F., and Addario, D. "A Comparison of Biofeedback-Mediated Relaxation and Group Therapy in the Treatment of Chronic Anxiety." *American Journal of Psychiatry,* 1975, *132,* 598–601.
Turk, D. E., Meichenbaum, D., and Genest, M. *Pain and Behavioral Medicine: A Cognitive-Behavioral Perspective.* New York: Guilford, 1983.
Wolpe, J. *The Practice of Behavior Therapy.* (3rd ed.) New York: Pergamon, 1982.

Wayne A. Bowers is a licensed staff psychologist in the clinical psychology division of the Department of Psychiatry at the University of Iowa.

The study of anxiety disorders in children is of interest both in its own right and for what it may reveal about the origins of anxiety disorders at any age.

Anxiety and Anxiety Disorder in Childhood

James H. L. Beeghly

Anxiety and fearfulness have been experienced by almost everyone, at least transiently, and are ubiquitous as symptoms in a wide variety of psychiatric disorders. The variety of experiences that are described as anxiety is great enough that one can legitimately ask whether anxiety is one phenomenon or many. When we discuss anxiety disorders in children, it is not always clear whether we are talking about unique disorders or about early-onset forms of corresponding adult disorders. Neither is it always clear which disorder should be included in this category. Sleep terror disorder, for example, has many symptoms in common with an anxiety attack but is now felt to be a parasomnia related to a specific stage of sleep.

Although it is impossible to define anxiety in a way that all would agree with, it is clear that anxiety causes a significant amount of pain and dysfunction among children. Surveys of large populations of children find a significant number of markedly anxious children. Rutter and others (1970, pp. 181-186) in a survey of over 200 ten- and eleven-year old children on the Isle of Wight found an overall corrected prevalence of psychiatric disorder of 6.8 percent. About one-third of these suffered from an anxiety disorder consisting primarily of anxiety, worrying, and general fearfulness. One-third of those with anxiety disorders had specific fears or phobias severe enough to be handicapping. A second group constituting

R. A. Muñoz (ed.). *Treating Anxiety Disorders.*
New Directions for Mental Health Services, no. 32. San Francisco: Jossey-Bass, Winter 1986.

about 0.4 percent of the total group of children had prominent obsessive symptoms as well as symptoms of anxiety. However, none of these children had a complete obsessional syndrome as seen in adults. Social phobia, agoraphobia, and hysteria (which some have also felt to be related to anxiety) were not seen in this age group.

Anxiety is a major problem among children seeking mental health services as well. Studies of typical patterns of symptoms in children attending child guidance clinics consistently identify one or more patterns of symptoms that correlate with anxiety (Hewitt and Jenkins, 1946; Collins and others, 1962; Patterson, 1964; Achenbach, 1966).

Understanding the continuities and discontinuities among developmentally normal fears and anxieties, childhood anxiety disorder, and adult anxiety disorder is of great importance for the treatment of anxious individuals of all ages. This chapter will focus on anxiety in prepubescent children, beginning with developmentally normal fears and anxieties, proceeding through descriptions of the clinical presentation and treatment of their anxiety disorders, and concluding by returning to the question of whether or not anxiety disorders in children are fundamentally different from anxiety disorders in adults.

Anxiety in Developmental Context

Developmentally Normal Anxieties in Infancy. There is some debate about the range of an infant's capacity to experience emotions at birth. Clearly, emotional development is linked to neurologic, perceptual, and cognitive development. During the first six months, an infant lacks the ability to anticipate having either positive or negative feelings based on previous experience. Specifically, anxiety and fear, based on anticipated distress, do not occur even in the case of physically painful possibilities. The infant may play with strangers as willingly as with its mother. Thus, the capacity to experience fear and anxiety seems to develop in the second half of the first year of life.

Somewhere between three and fifteen months, an infant becomes *attached* to specific people. Usually this is one person, in particular its mother (Rutter, 1981a, p. 269), and the infant is upset at her absence. The various proposed explanations of attachment form a major part of developmental theory and cannot be considered in detail here. Attachment is a complex phenomenon that can be demonstrated in the young of many species and appears to be at least partly biologically determined (Rajecki and others, 1978). Its importance to this discussion lies, first of all, in the fact that an infant is able to reduce anxiety and tension and, correspondingly, to increase inquisitive exploration porportionally to the strength and security of attachment. There is evidence that the quality of attachment affects later social relationships (Rutter, 1981a, p. 273-274).

Of particular interest is the concept of "anxious attachment"

(Bowlby, 1973, p. 213). This term refers to a tendency, first seen during early childhood, for some individuals to cling possessively to important adults, their "attachment figures." It is postulated that children come to "forecast" the likelihood of an attachment figure being accessible and willing to help based on their early experiences and that, after about age fifteen, the forecast is relatively fixed. Anxious attachment is felt to be the result of an individual having no confidence that his attachment figures will be available when needed if he does not stay close.

Normal separation anxiety (unlike the psychiatric disorder of the same name) begins around six months, peaks around eighteen months, and gradually fades away over the next couple of years (Rutter, 1981b, p. 309). When mother leaves, the infant will first try to follow, call out for her return, cry, and then become relatively subdued. The severity and duration of separation anxiety are related to the security of the infant's attachment to mother but also to the infant's cognitive ability to realize that the separation is temporary.

The development of fear of strangers at approximately eight months of age is closely related to both separation anxiety and the ability to form attachments but is not identical to either. (Although fear and anxiety are not truly synonymous—the former indicating a "response to an actual, current danger" most frequently "to the physical integrity of the individual" and the latter suggesting a response to an "impending threat to the personality in the context of the social environment" (Kolb and Brodie, 1982, p. 93)—the distinction is often quite difficult without a detailed description of how the individual perceives a given threat. The two words are, thus, often used interchangeably.) The infant begins with a wariness toward strangers indicated by frowns, worried face, averted gaze, and more rapid heartbeat. During the next few months, there is often crying and fearful behavior whenever strangers approach.

Developmentally normal separation anxiety produces very similar symptoms to those seen in separation anxiety disorder in older children and young adults. Similarly, fear of strangers and strange situations in the infant resembles the behavior of the child with avoidant disorders of childhood and adolescence. Children with either disorder are quite likely to feel much more comfortable with their mother and immediate family than they are with other people but still want to be liked and have friends.

We are still learning about the complicated interactions between child, parent, and environment that govern the early stages of development. It is not entirely clear whether the increasing ability to be away from mother that occurs as a child progresses through normal development represents a decrease in the strength of the attachment bond—attachment presumably having served its purpose in development and being no longer necessary—or an increase in that strength—the bond having become so dependable that the child can feel safe being away from mother for increasing periods of time (Rutter, 1981a, p. 273). The exact relationship between separation anxiety disorder and the quality of the attachment bond during these early years is unknown. Bowlby (1973, p. 300) has suggested that separation anxiety may be linked to the development of agoraphobia in adults. Gittleman and Klein (1984) find support for this hypothesis based on the recollections of agoraphobic adults, various family studies, and similarities in response to treatment.

Temperament. The discussion so far has implied that one infant is pretty much like another. There is good evidence that this is not entirely true. Chess and Thomas (1984), with the New York Longitudinal Study, have followed several children from the early neonatal period to young adulthood and have developed an interactional "goodness of fit" theory of the development of behavior disorders in children that has achieved a large measure of acceptance. The central tenet of this model is that an infant has innately determined tendencies to react to both internal and external events in certain ways, recognizable as "temperament" by two to three months. While some patterns of temperament lend more vulnerability to developing disorder than others, the ultimate outcome of a child with a given temperament depends on how well the environment "fits" that temperament; that is, whether the child is presented with situations that it is reasonably capable of handling.

Chess and Hassibi, (1978, p. 96-97) have suggested that temperament may help determine what type of symptoms a child develops when overly stressed and that children with a particular pattern of temperament, Slow-to-Warm-up, may be more prone than others to develop anxiety, avoidant behavior, and low self-esteem. The Slow-to-Warm-up child is described as shy but capable of enjoying and participating in new situations if given an opportunity for gradual approach. Temperamental characteristics of the Slow-to-Warm-up pattern include biological irregularity, predominance of negative mood, withdrawing reactions to new stimuli, slow adaptability, but only mild intensity of expressiveness (Chess and Hassibi, 1978, p. 92-93). This type of youngster may be at particular risk for school phobia (Chess and Hassibi, 1978, p. 97).

Normal Fears of Childhood. Rutter (1981b, p. 310) places the peak prevalence of specific fears at two to four years, with different types of fears being more prominent at different ages. Fear of noises, falling, and strange objects peak before age two and are largely absent by the time children are starting school. Fear of animals peak around three years followed by peaks in fear of the dark and fear of imaginary creatures over the next few years. Some specific fears, such as fear of snakes, while common and essentially normal, have no specific age of peak frequency. Bauer (1976) compared children in kindergarten and second and sixth grade and found that, with increasing age, fears of animals and imaginary creatures were progressively replaced by fear of bodily harm.

Lapouse and Monk (1959) used questionnaires to examine the types and prevalences of fears in a weighted representative sample of Buffalo, New York, children, aged six to twelve. Seven or more specific fears were found in 43 percent of the children, 48 percent of those six to eight and 37 percent of those nine to twelve. Various behaviors that had been thought to be related to fearfulness, such as bed wetting, nail biting, thumb sucking, teeth grinding and so on, did not turn out to be more common among the children with relatively more fears. Girls were significantly more likely to have a larger number of fears than were boys.

Miller and others (1972) subjected parent ratings on a fear inventory for children aged six to sixteen to factor analysis and found three main categories: fear of natural or supernatural events (storms, the dark, and so on), fear of injury, and fear of psychic stress (fear of mistakes, fear of making others angry, and the like). Comparing their work to studies of adults they concluded that fears of injury and fears of psychic stress often continued through much of the life span, whereas fears of natural events tended to diminish greatly after childhood.

Presenting Symptoms. It has been found useful to distinguish between symptoms related to the acute experience of overwhelming anxiety, that is, a "state" of anxiety, and symptoms related to chronic feelings of anxiety, referred to as the "trait" of anxiety or "anxiousness" (Lader, 1972, p. 481). State and trait anxiety are obviously related, and the frequent experience of anxiety states such as occurs in panic disorder may be associated with or possibly causal of pervasive, anticipatory anxiety and avoidance, suggestive of trait anxiety.

An example of a nine-year-old boy, with normal intelligence, who came to medical attention because of refusal to go to school illustrates a variety of symptoms, both acute and chronic. John began having problems going to school in the second grade following a quarrel with another student and "getting yelled at" by a teacher. He was fine on weekends or evenings but felt progressively worse as the time to leave for school approached. He often complained of being sick and having a stomachache before school. As he physically approached school, he progressed from looking discouraged and frowning to trembling, palpitations, crying, disorientation, and frantically clinging to his mother. He described feeling as if there was an "invisible wall" between him and the school. Once in school and settled at his desk, however, he calmed down and had no further problems. John had or had had a number of other feared situations, including being in the dark, accidentally being locked in or trapped inside a building or house, and the possibility of death for himself or his parents. Socially, he was initially shy, but could eventually relax and have a good time.

To what extent does a child's experience of anxiety differ from an adult's? Although there are no specific studies, a comparison of symptom lists for anxiety in children (Behar and Stewart, 1981) and for anxiety in adults (Goodwin and Guze, 1984, p. 72) suggests that physiological symptoms are not greatly different. On the other hand, the former authors note (p. 348–349) that anxious "prepubertal children, especially the younger ones," may experience more parasympathetic nervous system symptoms compared to anxious adolescents and adults who may have "sympathetic nervous system overactivity."

Lader suggests (1972, p. 486) that "although the experience of anxiety is innate, the use of the correct words to describe the feeling is a learned skill." More recently, the concept of alexithymia, "literally meaning 'no words for mood,' has been applied to a group of 'people who lack an ability to describe their feelings verbally,' who seem unable to fantasize, and who report multiple somatic symptoms" (Lesser, 1985). If one must learn to conceptualize one's feelings and put them into words and if lack of this ability in some way inhibits the ability to subjectively experience them, then it may be that all children go through an "alexithymic" stage and that some persist in this longer than others. By analogy, one could speculate that this would make a child relatively more likely to present (and therefore experience?) anxiety as a physical sensation or symptom. It has been noted that anxious children are often first brought to a physician's attention by one of a variety of somatic complaints (Stewart and Gath, 1978).

Clinical Anxiety Disorders

Issues of Classification. Before discussing specific syndromes, it is necessary to discuss the issue of diagnosis. Prior to the development of the present *Diagnostic and Statistical Manual of Mental Disorders* (DSM-III) of the American Psychiatric Association, disabling anxiety was generally discussed under the heading of neurosis. Under DSM-III the unifying concept of neurosis is no longer endorsed, and the various syndromes that had been classified under this theory of causation are now classified according to the observed pattern of symptoms. DSM-III includes a larger number of diagnoses than either of the earlier systems and is relatively more specific about criteria that must be met to make a given diagnosis. While there are many advantages to this approach, it has produced several categories of disorder that directly or indirectly involve anxiety where previously there had been only a few such categories.

There are relatively few research papers that are organized around these specific categories. Rutter and Shaffer (1980) have criticized DSM-III for including diagnoses such as avoidant disorder of childhood and adolescence, which have almost no justification in research, while failing to provide a residual category of childhood anxiety disorder for cases that do not clearly fit into one of the more explicitly defined categories, and for failing to acknowledge that many children have mixed emotional disorders rather than discrete disorders.

In DSM-III an anxiety disorder is one in which anxiety is either the predominant disturbance or is experienced if the individual attempts to master the symptoms (to resist a compulsion, for example). The diagnosis of anxiety disorder is not made if another disorder, such as schizophrenia, that could explain the anxiety is present.

Disorders Usually First Evident in Infancy, Childhood, or Adolescence

Three anxiety disorders are felt to begin (and often end) in childhood:

Separation Anxiety Disorder. This is a syndrome of excessive anxiety on separation from major attachment figures or from home or other familiar surroundings. When separation occurs, the child may experience anxiety to the point of panic. It must be a reaction beyond that expected at the child's developmental level. The age of onset may be as early as preschool, but the extreme form, involving school refusal, occurs most commonly around ages eleven to twelve. The symptoms of this "not uncommon" disorder may wax and wane over several years. Affected children often come from families that are close-knit and caring, are equally likely to be male or female, and, typically, develop symptoms after some life stress. Separation anxiety shows some tendency to run in families.

Overanxious Disorder. This is a pattern of generalized and persistent anxiety or worry (not related to concerns about separation), as demonstrated by the presence of at least four of seven key symptoms for least six months. Onset may be gradual or sudden and is said to be more common in eldest children of either sex, members of small families, families of higher socioeconomic status, and families overly concerned with competitive success. It is not clear whether increased risk for this disorder can be inherited.

Avoidant Disorder of Childhood and Adolescence. Children with this disorder suffer persistent and excessive shrinking from contact with strangers, of sufficient severity to interfere with social functioning in peer relationships, coupled with a clear desire for affection and acceptance. Relationships with family members and other familiar figures are warm and satisfying. The diagnosis is said to occur in children as young as two-and-a-half (after stranger anxiety should have disappeared) and follow a variable course, although it is thought to be relatively uncommon for it to persist into an adult avoidant personality disorder.

Anxiety Disorders Not Specific to Childhood

Of all the diagnostic categories in the "Anxiety Disorders" section of DSM-III only generalized anxiety disorder has a specific minimum age, eighteen. Nevertheless, many of the other diagnoses in this category are made infrequently in children. Simple phobias, however, are common at all ages.

Simple Phobias. Although isolated fear is considered normal at certain stages of development, when it occurs far enough beyond its normal developmental age range, or when it causes enough distress, it is considered to be a simple or specific phobia. However, the boundary between fear and phobia is not always clear. DSM-III defines a simple phobia as a "persistent, irrational fear of, and compelling desire to avoid, an object or a situation other than being alone, or in public places away from home (agoraphobia), or of humiliation or embarrassment in certain social situations (social phobia)" (p. 229).

Phobia is separated from ordinary fears by the fact that the afflicted individual is able to recognize that this particular fear is unreasonable or excessive. To meet DSM-III criteria it must not be due to another mental disorder. Simple phobia is the most common type of phobic disorder in the general population, though not the most common among those that present for treatment. Symptoms occur with a severity that is proportional to the phobic individual's proximity to the feared object or situation. Sudden direct exposure may cause symptoms identical to a panic attack.

Animal phobias are most clearly associated with childhood onset. Age of onset of situational phobias spans a wide range but most commonly falls in adulthood (Marks and Gelder, 1966). Some specific objects or situations, snakes and heights, for example, are much more common as phobic stimuli than others (Agras and others, 1969), leading to the hypothesis that some stimuli are especially potent inducers of phobia.

Simple phobias often occur along with other anxiety disorders. Agras and others (1972) studied the natural course of untreated phobias in adults and children under fourteen. At five-year follow-up 40 percent of the children were symptom free versus 6 percent of the adults. While all of the children had had at least some reduction in severity of phobia at follow-up, 37 percent of adults actually had worsening of symptoms. The distribution of the different types of fears is not given according to age, but it seems likely that it was not identical for the two age groups and that this accounted for some of the difference.

Animal phobias had the best outcome and also typically had the earliest onset. The authors also note that generalized phobias, those with a greater variety of potential objects to induce fear, such as injury phobias, tended to have a worse prognosis than relatively specific phobias, such as fear of heights.

While simple phobias have been treated based on insight-oriented psychoanalytic methods, the most common and effective methods are based on desensitization techniques derived from learning theory. These methods are also used with all types of phobia and obsessive-compulsive disorder.

Learning theory suggest that anxiety can be triggered by a previously neutral stimulus if that stimulus has become associated, because of a person's previous experience, with a noxious stimulus. Ordinarily, this association will not continue indefinitely without periodic demonstration of the connection between the "conditioned" and "unconditioned" stimuli. However, because simply approaching or even thinking about the conditioned stimulus causes anxiety, it is phobically avoided (Wolpe, 1981). There is, thus, no chance to "unlearn" or extinguish the association. The recollections of phobic adults suggest that such conditioned phobic responses may be engendered from even one traumatic event (Öst and Hugdahl, 1981). Although this model has proven inadequate to explain phobias completely, especially those other than simple phobias (Rachman, 1977), it has generated a number of useful treatments designed to help the patient overcome avoidance of the feared object or situation and thus "learn" that it is innocuous.

Systematic desensitization involves first training a patient in relaxation techniques, then exposing the patient to stimuli that are progressively more anxiety-provoking. Each time the patient begins to feel anxious, relaxation is induced. If a child is afraid of dogs, the child might be asked to imagine a series of situations that were closer and closer to petting the dog—in vitro desensitization—or to actually come closer and closer to the dog—in vivo desensitization. It is likely that the latter method is more effective (Ultee and others, 1982).

Modeling attempts to reduce anxiety by having the patient observe someone else engage in the anxiety-provoking activity and is a technique that may be especially useful with a child. Bandura and Menlove (1968) used films depicting models displaying progressively more relaxed interactions with dogs to treat animal phobias in a group of three-to-five-year-olds. Modeling may be combined with participation. Thus, an alternative method of dealing with an animal phobia would be having a trusted adult first model with a stuffed animal, then physically guide a child through successive steps in approaching and finally petting a dog (Matson, 1983).

Flooding is the process of putting a patient in direct contact with the feared stimulus for however long it takes for the extreme anxiety that results to abate. While obviously not applicable to all cases of phobia, this technique may be one of the most effective of the behavioral techniques. Yule and others (1974) successfully treated an eleven-year-old boy with a severe noise phobia in two sessions. He remained free of phobic behavior over a twenty-five month period. In clinical practice the various behavioral methods are often used in combination with each other and with systems of rewards for desired behavior (Bornstein and Knapp, 1981; Esveldt-Dawson and others, 1982).

Obsessive-Compulsive Disorder in Childhood. DSM-III defines this as a disorder in which obsessions or compulsions must be present, not due to another mental disorder, and a source of significant distress. No age criteria is specified, but the disorder, accounting for less than 5 percent of adult psychiatric patients (Goodwin and Guze, 1984, p. 111), is considered to be even less common in childhood. Chess and Hassibi (1978, p. 250) suggest that this disorder accounts for about one percent of child psychiatric referrals and that the onset of symptoms is between the ages of six and ten. Rapoport and others (1981) cite evidence that the prevalence is even lower. However, studies of adults with this disorder suggest that as many as a third of them had onset of symptoms in childhood or early adolescence (Hersov, 1985a, p. 375). Afflicted children are more likely to be male and of average or better intelligence.

Repetitive rituals such as avoiding stepping on sidewalk cracks, engaging in nonsense rhymes, or tapping alternate light poles are considered a part of normal play (Marks, 1981, p. 180; Judd, 1965, p. 137–138) but are generally transitory phenomena that do not involve much anxiety. Obsessive-compulsive disorder is generally distinguished from personality traits that resemble it by the fact that individuals with the former condition actively resist these thoughts or urges to action (Judd, 1965, p. 136).

Obsessive-compulsive disorder has been described by Rapoport and others (1981, p. 1545) as unique in that "the symptoms and clinical picture of the childhood disorder are virtually identical to those of adult patients." Hersov, on the other hand, has suggested (1985a, p. 375) that "unlike the adult, the obsessional child usually does not or cannot always keep his thoughts or compulsions to himself." Active resistance against obsessions and compulsions is often hard to assess in a young child and may not be essential to the diagnosis in this group.

There is some disagreement about family backgrounds and mode of onset. Studies based on children seen at clinics (Judd, 1965; Hollingsworth and others, 1980) suggest that psychopathology, and specifically obsessive-compulsive disorder, is quite common in immediate relatives of obsessive-compulsive children. Onset was described as frequently sudden, often following a frightening event. Feelings of guilt were frequently expressed. In contrast, Rapoport and others (1981), studying subjects who were recruited through advertisement rather than by selection from a clinic or inpatient population, found little evidence of a specific type or excess of parental psychopathology or of specific premorbid personality features. The authors noted that family conflict in several cases seemed to have been caused by the child's symptoms, rather than the reverse.

There is evidence, including twin studies, that obsessive-compulsive disorder is more common among relatives of afflicted individuals than in the general population (Goodwin and Guze, 1984, p. 111). However, none of the twin series involves twins raised apart. There are no adoption studies either. Thus, the effects of environment and heredity have not been completely disentangled. Chess and Hassibi (1978, p. 252) suggest that families that discourage affective expression and make love and acceptance contingent upon meeting strict standards may contribute to perfectionism and anxiety and guilt over failures but point out that many such families do not produce obsessive-compulsive children.

Probably due to the fact that obsessive-compulsive disorder is not at all frequently identified in children, nearly all treatment studies have been done with adults. The traditional method of treatment is insight-oriented psychotherapy aimed at uncovering intrapsychic conflict. More recently, behavioral modification methods based on learning theory have been employed with somewhat better effect. The underlying theory is that obsessions and compulsions are comparable to phobic avoidance and are, similarly, maintained because they reduce anxiety. Thus, the behavioral methods described in the treatment of phobias—desensitization, modeling, and flooding—have all been employed, often with response prevention—not allowing compulsive rituals to be performed—as well.

Pharmacotherapy with antidepressants, particularly chlorimipramine, has achieved some success in adult forms of the disorder (Insel and Murphy, 1981; Ananth, 1983). There are relatively few studies of such treatment in children. Rapoport and others (1980) were unable to demonstrate a positive effect of chlorimipramine in a small group of adolescents. However, Bolton and others (1983) treated 15 adolescents with a combination of response prevention and chlorimipramine and obtained at least some improvement in 13. While behavioral methods are probably most successful at treating compulsions and less effective or even ineffective in reducing associated symptoms, such as depression or free-floating anxiety (Beech and Vaughan, 1978,p. 75), pharmacotherapy may be most successful when depressive or anxiety symptoms are present (Marks, 1983). Further research on the use of antidepressants in childhood obsessive-compulsive disorder is clearly needed.

Warren (1960) concluded from a long-term follow-up study of a pediatric population with obsessive-compulsive disorder that complete recovery occurred only 50 percent of the time. Many obsessive-compulsive children will manage to continue functioning although still symptomatic. Hollingsworth and others (1980) were able to locate and interview 10 of 17 children originally identified by chart review at an average of 6.5 years after last contact. Although all of them were doing well in school, only 3 of the 10 denied any obsessive-compulsive symptoms.

It is of considerable theoretical interest that children with Gilles de la Tourette syndrome may present with symptoms that are very difficult to distinguish from obsessive-compulsive disorder (Nee and others, 1980). Shapiro and others (1978, p. 255–256) acknowledge that a small group of Tourette's patients have "obsessive and compulsive-like phenomena" but suggest that these "fantasies" differ from those of patients who truly have obsessive-compulsive disorder in that "no single fantasy persists for long" and compulsive and phobic personality traits are not usually seen.

Others would suggest that obsessive-compulsive symptoms occur in as many as one-third of Tourette's patients and that compulsivity is a common personality characteristic (Valzelli, 1982, p. 208–209). While it is, of course, possible for an individual to have two separate disorders, the relative prevalences of these two disorders would not allow chance association to explain very many cases of both disorders occurring in one person. The following case is, perhaps, a better illustration of obsessive-compulsive disorder than it is of Tourette's syndrome, though the latter is the primary diagnosis.

Arnold first received attention for tics and noises in the fourth grade. There was an excess of nervous snorting, raising his eyebrows, turning his head and rolling his eyes as early as kindergarten. By the time of his fourth-grade evaluation he was also making "honking" noises, sometimes as often as several per minute. At age twelve, obsessive ruminations about death developed following an attack of angina in his father and a six-month absence by his mother to attend a dying sister. By age fourteen, tics and noises had worsened. However, he was more distressed by his ruminations. He was constantly afraid that some thought that he had would anger God and that he would be the cause of harm to someone because of his thoughts. He would cough paroxysmally every time his mother lit a cigarette, convinced she would die of cancer. He constantly demanded reassurances and felt compelled to pray every time he had a thought that might be displeasing to God. Treatment with haloperidol readily improved the tics and noises but was less effective with the obsessive-compulsive symptoms.

Despite the relationship to obsessive-compulsive disorder, Tourette's Syndrome might not merit mention in a chapter on anxiety were it not for the fact that there have been recent reports of separation anxiety and school refusal "indistinguishable from DSM-III criteria" developing in some Tourette's children when treated with haloperidol or primozide (Mikkelsen and others, 1981; Linet, 1985).

Panic Disorder in Children. DSM-III (APA, 1980, p. 230) gives the age of onset as "late adolescence or early adult life," but there is evidence that it may begin much earlier. Sheehan and others (1981) obtained histories of age of onset from one hundred adults diagnosed as having panic disorder. Fourteen percent of them dated the onset to fourteen years or younger. Four percent dated the onset to nine or younger. These authors argue that panic disorder is a single entity with a broad range of age of onset.

There is strong evidence for a genetic contribution to panic disorder separate from other types of anxiety (Crowe and others, 1983; Goodwin and Guze, 1984, pp. 78–79; Anderson and others, 1984). This being the case, it would seem to follow that at least the seeds of the disorder are present in childhood. Van Winter and Stickler (1984) describe a twelve-year-old boy who began to have panic attacks at age eight and represented the fourth generation of panic disorder in his family.

Of interest because it has been studied in children, hyperventilation syndrome (HVS)—a collection of psychosomatic symptoms such as tingling, numbness, sweating, lightheadedness, heart palpitations, difficulty getting a breath, extreme anxiety, perceptual alterations, and even hallucinations brought on by physiological changes caused, in turn, by rapid breathing—produces symptoms that are very similar to panic disorder and has an unclear relationship to it (Goodwin and Guze, 1984, p. 82–83). Hyperventilation may or may not accompany panic attacks. While, theoretically, anyone could develop HVS from overbreathing long enough, those who actually develop the syndrome appear to have first developed a pattern of frequent sighing (Lewis, 1979). There may also be variation in individual vulnerability. Thus, as few as five deep breaths may be enough to trigger symptoms (Christensen, 1946).

HVS appears to occur in individuals with a variety of psychiatric disorders or no psychiatric disorder at all. Herman and others (1981) examined the records of 34 individuals with HVS who had been less than eighteen when first seen and classified them into five categories. Type 1 displayed chronic and acute signs of anxiety. Type 2 was termed "idiopathic." Type 3 patients had histories suggestive of pronounced psychopathology or severely disturbed family situations or both. Type 4 patients displayed the syndrome only in response to certain clearly stressful events. Type 5 individuals hyperventilated only after rigorous physical activity. Half of the children had had prior medical problems resulting in long hospitalizations. A quarter of the children had had previous psychiatric diagnoses.

Follow-up information was obtained on 30 of these children after periods of time ranging from two to twenty-eight years. Forty percent of these individuals continued to suffer HVS; 50 percent continued to have anxiety symptoms. Unfortunately, these figures are not broken down according to the typology originally described above. It is unclear whether these with chronic HVS would have met criteria for panic disorder.

Treatment of panic disorder in adults has blossomed with the discovery of the effectiveness of several classes of medication, including the various tricyclics, monoamine oxidase inhibitors, propranolol, and alprazolam. There are very few such studies, as yet, in children. Van Winter and Stickler (1984) describe 7 patients, aged nine to seventeen, with the specific diagnosis of panic disorder. Two did well with reassurance alone. Four had been started on imipramine. One had had to stop due to side effects and remained symptomatic. A second child did not respond and had to be switched to propranolol, which was effective. The seventh child had mitral valve prolapse and tachycardia and did well with intermittent propranolol. Panic disorder may well be closely related to separation anxiety disorder, so that the successful use of imipramine in this disorder by Gittelman-Klein and Klein (1971) would be relevant.

School Refusal. School refusal is not diagnosis but, rather, a cardinal symptom of underlying problems, capable of galvanizing parents, school, social workers, and psychiatrists into action. It is a syndrome in which a child is effectively prevented from attending school by extremely disturbing emotions, usually fear and anxiety. While no single psychiatric diagnosis corresponds to school refusal, many children would be diagnosed as having a separation anxiety disorder under DSM-III. Hersov, (1985b) has traced the evolution of the concept referred to as "school phobia" or "school refusal," beginning with Broadwin's (1932) description of children who were miserable and fearful at school but happy at home. Hersov emphasizes the distinction between truancy, which is often but one indication of conduct disorder, and school refusal, which occurs "against the background of a variety of psychiatric disorders" (p. 383).

Kennedy (1965) indicated that school phobia occurred at the rate of 17 cases per thousand school-age children per year, without specifying the source of this figure. In contrast, Rutter and others (1970, p. 183) found no cases in which school refusal was either the chief or a persisting problem in a survey of 2193 rural ten- and eleven-year-olds. It seems likely that the prevalence will vary considerably from place to place. School refusal accounts for 1 to 8 percent of cases seen in a child guidance or child psychiatry clinic, with highest prevalences at ages five to seven, eleven, and fourteen or over (Hersov, 1985b, p. 384–385). Perhaps not surprisingly, given the heterogeneity of the syndrome, there is disagreement about whether school refusal is preferentially associated with a particular sex, birth order, or social class (Baker and Wills, 1978; McDonald and Sheperd, 1976).

In a recent review Atkinson and others (1985) present the major theories that have been advanced to explain school refusal, as well as a discussion of significant subgroups within the syndrome. They conclude that four groups of school refusers may be distinguished according to the main source of fear: fear of separation, fear of failure, fear of failure in the school situation, and general fearfulness. Alternatively, children with this syndrome may be divided into those with relatively acute onset after several trouble-free years and those with more general dysfunction in which fear of school was a part of a more general fearfulness of the outside world—termed, respectively, "neurotic" and "characterological" by Coolidge and others (1957) or "Type 1" and "Type 2" by Kennedy (1965).

Atkinson and others (1985) concluded that children in the characterological group tend to be older and more disturbed and to come from the lower socioeconomic classes compared to the neurotic group. School refusers in the characterological group are less likely to have had a clear precipitating factor in their school refusal and are less amenable to treatment. It has been argued that separation concerns are more relevant to the younger, neurotic group.

The parents of school refusers are often caught up in the problem. Psychiatric illness is more common in the parents of school refusal children than in the population in general, though not necessarily more common or different in type than in the parents of children receiving psychiatric treatment for other reasons (Berg and others, 1974; Berg and others, 1981). Breit (1982), on the other hand, found that mothers of children with separation anxiety differed from mothers of children with behavior disorders on responses to the Thematic Apperception Test. Stories by the former group expressed significantly more concerns about abandonment and rejection and more often expressed a desire to stay near the loved one.

Because of the importance of family variables, school refusal has also been subdivided according to family interactions. Bowlby (1973, p. 264) derived four patterns of family interaction from a review of the literature. In the first pattern, one parent, usually mother, suffers chronic anxiety regarding attachment figures and keeps the child home as a companion. He felt that this was the most common pattern and that it was also often combined with any of the other three. In the second pattern the child fears something dreadful will happen to a parent, again usually mother, and stays home to prevent it from happening. Children with the third type of family fear something terrible will happen to themselves if they are away from home. In the fourth pattern, a parent, usually mother, fears something dreadful will happen to the child at school, specifically.

Hersov (1960, p. 40) combined parent and child variables to describe three patterns of parent-child relationships: one in which there is an overindulgent mother, an inadequate, passive father, and a child who is usually timid and inhibited away from home but willful and stubborn at home; a second one in which there is a controlling, demanding mother, a passive father, and a child who is timid and fearful away from home and passive and obedient at home; and a final pattern in which there is an overindulgent mother, a firm, controlling father who is active at home, and a child who is outgoing and friendly away from home but stubborn, demanding, and closely bound to the mother at home.

If one attempts to apply the DSM-III diagnostic system to any of the subclassifications above, the best fit may be between the neurotic pattern and separation anxiety disorder. Characterological children, who are more generally fearful and withdrawn, may fit into the category of avoidant disorder of childhood and adolescence. Children who are particularly fearful of failure or of the school situation may fit into the overanxious disorder category.

As a matter of course, the various physical disorders that can masquerade behind anxiety symptoms (Behar and Stewart, 1981) should be screened for before moving to psychological concerns. Given the varied nature of school refusal, it follows that treatment should begin with a careful assessment of the relevant factors in a particular child's patterns of school refusal. Depending on the main focus of concern, treatment with one or several different techniques ranging from alteration of the external environment through changes at school to alteration of the internal environment with pharmacotherapy may be indicated. Use of multiple techniques is common.

Kennedy's treatment of an uncomplicated case, for example, involves techniques of flooding and selective reinforcement of desired behavior along with some alteration of the home and school environments. School officials and parents are trained to get the child to school and keep him there, forcibly if necessary, while pairing minimal attention to somatic complaints and maximum attention to success in attending school. A hint of family therapy is invoked as father is drawn into a more active role in physically getting the child to school while mother is required to be less involved and may "stand in the hall, if she must, or . . . visit the school during the morning, but not to stay" (Kennedy, 1965, p. 288).

Physical complaints such as stomach pain and headaches often peak as the time to leave for school approaches and reflect real, if momentary, distress. Quite commonly an otherwise resolute parent is overwhelmed with guilt and cannot insist. Rules for what will constitute sickness (and will merit a trip to the doctor) may be set up. Often one parent will be more capable of remaining relatively unemotional in such a situation and should be designated as the one in charge of getting the children on their way to school.

Generally, the longer a child has been away from school, the harder it is to start back. Thus, most authors emphasize return to school as soon as possible. Supplementing Kennedy's method of, essentially, forcing a child back to school are several methods of making it more inviting for him to return. It is often useful to recruit another child from the neighborhood to walk with a child who is having difficulty going to school. If possible, a teacher, counselor, or principal may be designated to become the child's special friend and advocate, sometimes meeting him as he arrives at school or attempting to alter particularly fear-inducing situations.

Although fairly drastic measures such as the threat of legal action under the truancy laws are sometimes required, the majority of school refusers can probably be successfully gotten back to school through outpatient treatment. Failure of outpatient treatment is, perhaps, the one clear indication for hospitalization. The most immediate effect of hospitalization will be to crystallize the separation anxieties of both child and parent. Getting parents of school refusers to leave their child in hospital, especially during the first week, can be a prodigious task. If this crisis is gotten through, there is an opportunity for a therapist to work with dysfunctional family dynamics. Since virtually all child psychiatry units include provision for teaching, hospitalization, in effect, gets a child back in a school environment quickly. Moreover, the child's behavior with teachers, other children, and classwork can be "placed under the microscope," so to speak, and the effects of various modifications assessed. Particular aspects of the patient's functioning, such as low self-esteem, specific phobias, or specific learning disabilities, can be targeted with appropriate therapeutic techniques. Depending on the intelligence and insight of a given child, a simplified form of instruction in rational analysis of emotions, similar to that advocated as cognitive therapy for adults, may be useful (Beck and others, 1985). As the end of the hospital stay approaches, passes may be given to begin the reintegration of the child into the home school. Finally, since hospitalization is almost always viewed as aversive by the youngster, the real possibility of having to return to hospital if he does not stay in school may be raised to make it seem "less easy" for a child to stay home.

There is some indication that antidepressant medication may be helpful in this group of children. Gittelman-Klein and Klein (1971) conducted a rigorous study of imipramine in a group of seven- to fifteen-year-old school refusers who had previously failed to return to school despite two weeks of nonpharmacological treatment and found that this medication, in rather high doses, doubled the rate of successful return to school compared to placebo. However, it is now felt that imipramine should not be used in doses greater than 5 mg/kg, as it was in some of the children in this study, due to significant cardiovascular side effects. A study of chlorimipramine versus placebo using doses judged to be equivalent to somewhat lower doses of imipramine than used by Gittelman-Klein and Klein (1971) found no specific treatment effect in getting school refusers back to school (Berney and others, 1981).

Although there are only a few studies involving small numbers of children, two reviews of pharmacological treatment of childhood anxiety suggest that there is some possibility that benzodiazepines, notably chlordiazepoxide (Librium), may be helpful in the treatment of childhood anxiety (Klein and others, 1980, p. 715; Werry and Aman, 1980, p. 180). D'Amato (1962) used this medication to treat a group of nine school phobic children and found that they returned to school significantly sooner compared to the clinical records of similar children. However, the numbers are small and the comparison group inadequately controlled. Overall, medication should be used cautiously with this disorder and as adjunctive rather than as primary treatment.

The prognosis of school refusal as summarized by Hersov (1985b, p. 393) is generally good, with a successful outcome in two-thirds or more of the cases. Baker and Wills (1979) found that outcome, as measured by work performance assessed after the age when school would normally be completed, in a group of school phobic children seen at a clinic was not affected by how long the child had been out of school or even whether or not the child had ever returned to school. This favorable picture for school refusers in general obscures the somewhat worse outcome of children older than eleven years and children who require hospitalization (two overlapping groups) found by some authors. Berg and others (1976) found that only one-third of a group of school phobic children were substantially or completely improved at an average of three years after discharge from in-patient treatment. Another third of the group continued to have neurotic symptoms but with minimal social limitations. The remainder continued to have symptoms of persistent severe emotional disturbance and social impairment.

Relationship Between Childhood and Adult Anxiety. Two related questions conclude this chapter on childhood anxiety and place this subject in context as a subset of anxiety disorders in general. First, are there common mechanisms in childhood and adult anxiety disorders? Second, is there reason to believe that interventions in childhood can prevent adult anxiety disorder?

In the absence of clearly understood causation for virtually all anxiety disorders it is difficult to say with any certainty whether two given anxiety syndromes, one seen in children, one in adolescents and adults, might have common origins. The best evidence for such an association would be the demonstration that children with a particular childhood anxiety disorder grow up to have a particular adult anxiety disorder.

There have been relatively few of the long-term follow-up studies required for such a demonstration, and they have tended to examine the broad category of neurosis or neurotic symptoms rather than specific anxiety syndromes. The vast majority of children seen for neurotic symptoms are not psychiatrically ill as adults (Robins, 1966; Michael and others, 1957). This does not rule out similar mechanisms for child and adult disorders, since the majority of adults seen for anxiety neurosis also do quite well at follow-up (Goodwin and Guze, 1984, p. 76).

There is evidence from follow-up studies that personality traits of shyness and withdrawal after the age of six are fairly stable and are predictors of adult psychopathology (Robins, 1979). Similarly, when psychiatric records of their early treatment were obtained, adults in treatment for depression and anxiety who had been seen as children by psychiatrists had had similar symptoms of anxiety, depression, and somatic complaints (Pritchard and Graham, 1966). As described in earlier sections, there is also evidence, less reliable because based only on adult recollections, that obsessive-compulsive disorder and panic disorder can begin at a quite early age—the latter possibly as separation anxiety—and persist into adulthood.

Evidence of a genetic relationship between adult and child forms of anxiety disorder would also be suggestive of common mechanisms. Rutter (1972, p. 9) has hypothesized that childhood neurotic disorders that persist into adulthood may be distinguished by "the presence of personality attributes which have an important genetic component." Disorders characterized by acute anxiety sypmtoms superimposed on otherwise normal functioning would be less likely to have a genetic component.

Several family studies have established that anxiety neurosis in general is a familial condition with a risk between 18 and 20 percent that a given first-degree relative will also be affected (Goodwin and Guze, 1984, p. 78). A recent twin study, distinguished by the fact of a relatively large sample and the use of specific DSM-III anxiety disorder categories, found twice the rate of concordance of monozygotic versus dizygotic twins for anxiety disorders overall. Anxiety disorders with panic attacks were more than five times as frequent in monozygotic as in dizygotic twins, while generalized anxiety disorder showed no increase in concordance (Torgersen, 1983), somewhat the opposite of what Rutter's theory would suggest.

Specific attempts to connect childhood anxiety disorders and adult anxiety disorders are quite uncommon. Gittelman and Klein (1984) have reviewed the evidence along these lines for a relationship between separation anxiety in the child and panic and agoraphobic disorder in the adult. Two studies of the offspring of adults with psychiatric disorder found increased frequencies of separation anxiety in the children of adults with agoraphobia (many also with panic attacks). A single study of parents of children with school phobia did not identify a relative increase in frequency of agoraphobia among the adults.

Demonstration of a common underlying biologic marker would be strong evidence of common mechanism for adult and child anxiety disorders. Unfortunately, the burgeoning anxiety research into physiology has not yet been applied to children. There are several chemically induced models of anxiety (Griez, 1984; Skolnick and others, 1984). The complicated relationship between benzodiazepine receptors, the neurotransmitter, GABA, and possible endogenous benzodiazepine-like compounds (Nesteros, 1984: Paul and others, 1980; Marx, 1984) is gradually being worked out. If this research into the physiology of anxiety can be extended to explain pathophysiology, there would be an excellent opportunity to compare child and adult anxiety disorders.

While preventing adult disorder could, arguably, be the most important goal of childhood anxiety disorder therapy, we have, as Rutter put it (1972, p. 3), "not a scrap of evidence" that this is possible. The concept of prevention implies not only continuity in some form between child and adult disorder but also the possibility of progression of disorder in some manner, if unchecked, so that it causes more dysfunction or becomes more difficult to treat. Certainly, there are some children, particularly those whose anxiety is a pervasive part of their personality, whose symptoms are most clearly age-inappropriate and seem least related to environmental stress, who do show both continuity and progression of anxiety (Rutter, 1972).

Despite the lack of demonstrable effect of childhood therapy on adult outcome, two points can be made in closing. First, despite the evidence of strong genetic contributions to some anxiety disorders, it is clear that environmental factors can have strong effects as well. The negative possibilities of environmental influence are vividly evident in a four-year follow-up study of 25 children suffering from post-traumatic stress syndrome after having been kidnapped and briefly buried alive (Terr, 1983). At the time of follow-up all of the children suffered from kidnap-related or other fears, as well as a variety of associated symptoms.

Second, it seems likely that positive environmental influences could be equally strong, if less dramatic. Childhood is, especially, a time of growth, of learning, and of developing adult patterns of behavior. A child whose experience is of frequent uncontrolled anxiety and fearfulness may learn that one must avoid all situations with the slightest risk. Risks not taken are challenges never overcome and "proof" to the child that he or she is a person who cannot do much and dare not take any chances. Evidence, provided by teaching (by parent, school counselor, or therapist) or example, that anxiety can be controlled or, at a minimum, lived with, as well as gentle but firm encouragement to carry through with slightly "risky" but potentially rewarding endeavors, may, at the very least, limit the development of secondarily acquired disability. Indeed, the good outcome of so many children with anxiety disorders suggests that such intervention is often all that is needed.

References

Achenbach, T. M. "The Classification of Children's Psychiatric Symptoms: A Factor-Analytic Study." *Psychology Monographs,* 1966, *80,* 1-37.

Agras, W. S., Chapin, H. N., Jackson, M., and Oliveau, D. C. "The Natural History of Phobia." *Archives of General Psychiatry,* 1972, *26,* 315-317.

Agras, W. S., Sylvester, D., and Oliveau, D. "The Epidemiology of Common Fears and Phobias." *Comprehensive Psychiatry,* 1969, *10,* 151-156.

American Psychiatric Association. *Diagnostic and Statistical Manual of Mental Disorders.* (3rd ed.) Washington, D.C.: American Psychiatric Association, 1980.

Ananth, J. "Clomipramine in Obsessive-Compulsive Disorder: A Review." *Psychosomatics,* 1983, *24* (8), 723-727.

Anderson, D. J., Noyes, R., and Crowe, R. R. "A Comparison of Panic Disorder and Generalized Anxiety Disorder." *American Journal of Psychiatry,* 1984, *141* (4), 572-575.

Atkinson, L., Quarrington, B., and Cyr, J. J. "School Refusal: The Heterogeneity of a Concept." *American Journal of Orthopsychiatry,* 1985, *55* (1), 83-101.

Baker, H., and Wills, U. "School Phobia: Classification and Treatment." *British Journal of Psychiatry,* 1978, *132,* 492-499.

Baker, H., and Wills, U. "School Phobic Children at Work." *British Journal of Psychiatry,* 1979, *135,* 561-564.

Bandura, A., and Menlove, F. L. "Factors Determining Vacarious Extinction of Avoidance Behavior Through Symbolic Modeling." *Journal of Personality and Social Psychology,* 1968, *8,* 99-108.

Bauer, D. H. "An Exploratory Study of Developmental Changes in Children's Fears." *Journal of Child Psychology and Psychiatry and Allied Disciplines,* 1976, *17,* 69-74.

Beck, A. T., and Emery, G., with Greenberg, R. *Anxiety Disorders and Phobias.* New York: Basic Books, 1985.

Beech, H. R., and Vaughan, M. *Behavioral Treatment of Obsessional States.* New York: Wiley, 1978.

Behar, D., and Stewart, M. A. "Anxiety." In S. Gabel (ed.), *Behavioral Problems in Childhood.* New York: Grune & Stratton, 1981.

Berg, I., Butler, A., Fairbairn, I., and McGuire, R. "The Parents of School Phobic Adolescents—A Preliminary Investigation of Family Life Variables." *Psychological Medicine,* 1981, *11,* 79–83.

Berg, I., Butler, A., and Hall, G. "The Outcome of Adolescent School Phobia." *British Journal of Psychiatry,* 1976, *128,* 80–85.

Berg, I., Butler, A., and Pritchard, J. "Psychiatric Illness in the Mothers of School-Phobic Adolescents." *British Journal of Psychiatry,* 1974, *125,* 466–467.

Berney, T., Kolvin, I., Bhate, S. R., Garside, R. F., Jeans, J., Kay, B., and Scarth, L. "School Phobia: A Therapeutic Trial with Clomipramine and Short-Term Outcome." *British Journal of Psychiatry,* 1981, *38,* 110–118.

Bolton, D., Collins, S., and Steinberg, D. "The Treatment of Obsessive-Compulsive Disorder in Adolescence." *British Journal of Psychiatry,* 1983, *142,* 456–464.

Bornstein, P. H., and Knapp, M. "Self-Control Desensitization with a Multi-Phobic Boy: A Multiple Baseline Design." *Journal of Behavior Therapy and Experimental Psychiatry,* 1981, *12* (3), 281–285.

Bowlby, J. *Attachment and Loss.* Vol. 2, *Separation Anxiety and Anger.* London: Hogarth, 1973.

Breit, M. "Separation Anxiety in Mothers of Latency-Age Fearful Children." *Journal of Abnormal Child Psychology,* 1982, *10* (1), 135–144.

Broadwin, I. T. "A Contribution to the Study of Truancy." *American Journal of Orthopsychiatry,* 1932, *2,* 253–259.

Chess, S., and Hassibi, M. *Principles and Practice of Child Psychiatry.* New York: Plenum, 1978.

Chess, S., and Thomas, A. *Origins and Evolution of Behavior Disorders from Infancy to Early Adult Life.* New York: Brunner/Mazel, 1984.

Christensen, B. "Studies on Hyperventilation. II: Electrocardiographic Changes in Normal Man During Voluntary Hyperventilation." *Journal of Clinical Investigation,* 1946, *24,* 880.

Collins, L. F., Maxwell, A. E., and Cameron, K. "A Factor Analysis of Some Child Psychiatric Clinic Data." *Journal of Mental Science,* 1962, *108,* 274–285.

Coolidge, J., Hahn, P., and Peck, A. "School Phobia: Neurotic Crisis or Way of Life." *American Journal of Orthopsychiatry,* 1957, *27,* 296–306.

Crowe, R. R., Noyes, R., Pauls, D. L., and Slymen, D. "A Family Study of Panic Disorder." *Archives of General Psychiatry,* 1983, *40* (10), 1065–1069.

D'Amato, G. "Chlordiazepoxide in Management of School Phobia." *Diseases of the Nervous System,* 1962, *23,* 293–295.

Esveldt-Dawson, S., Wisner, K. L., Unis, A. S., Matson, J. L., and Kazdin, A. E. "Treatment of Phobias in a Hospitalized Child." *Journal of Behavior Therapy and Experimental Psychiatry,* 1982, *13* (1), 77–83.

Gittelman-Klein, R., and Klein, D. F. "Controlled Imipramine Treatment of School Phobia." *Archives of General Psychiatry,* 1971, *25,* 204–207.

Gittelman, R., and Klein, D. F. "Relationship Between Separation Anxiety and Panic and Agoraphobic Disorders." *Psychopathology,* 1984, *17* (suppl. 1), 56–65.

Goodwin, D. W., and Guze, S. B. *Psychiatric Diagnosis.* (3rd ed.) New York: Oxford University Press, 1984.

Griez, E. "Experimental Models of Anxiety." *Acta Psychiatrica Belgica,* 1984, *84,* 511–532.

Herman, S. P., Stickler, G. B., and Lucas, A. R. "Hyperventilation Syndrome in

Children and Adolescents: Long-Term Follow-up." *Pediatrics,* 1981, *67* (2), 183-187.
Hersov, L. "Refusal to Go to School." *Journal of Child Psychology and Psychiatry,* 1960, *1,* 137-145.
Hersov, L. "Emotional Disorders." In M. Rutter and L. Hersov (eds.), *Child and Adolescent Psychiatry: Modern Approaches.* (2nd ed.) Boston: Blackwell Scientific Publications, 1985a.
Hersov, L. "School Refusal." In M. Rutter and L. Hersov (eds.), *Child and Adolescent Psychiatry: Modern Approaches.* (2nd ed.) Boston: Blackwell Scientific Publications, 1985b.
Hewitt, L., and Jenkins, R. L. *Fundamental Patterns of Maladjustment.* Springfield: State of Illinois, 1946.
Hollingsworth, C. E., Tanguay, P. E., Grossman, L., and Pabst, P. "Long-Term Outcome of Obsessive-Compulsive Disorder in Childhood." *Journal of the American Academy of Child Psychiatry,* 1980, *19,* 134-144.
Insel, T. R., and Murphy, D. L. "The Psychopharmacological Treatment of Obsessive-Compulsive Disorder: A Review." *Journal of Clinical Psychopharmacology,* 1981, *5,* 304-311.
Judd, L. "Obsessive-Compulsive Neurosis in Children." *Archives of General Psychiatry,* 1965, *12,* 136-143.
Kennedy, W. A. "School Phobia: Rapid Treatment of Fifty Cases." *Journal of Abnormal Psychology,* 1965, *70,* 285-289.
Klein, D. F., Gittelman, R., Quitkin, F., and Rifkin, A. *Diagnosis and Drug Treatment of Psychiatric Disorders: Adults and Children.* (2nd ed.) Baltimore: Williams and Wilkins, 1980.
Kolb, L. C., and Brodie, H.K.H. *Modern Clinical Psychiatry.* (10th ed.) Philadelphia: W. B. Saunders, 1982.
Lader, M. "The Nature of Anxiety." *British Journal of Psychiatry,* 1972, *121,* 481-491.
Lapouse, R., and Monk, M. "Fears and Worries in a Representative Sample of Children." *American Journal of Orthopsychiatry,* 1959, *29,* 803-818.
Lesser, I. M. "Alexithymia." *New England Journal of Medicine,* 1985, *312* (11), 690.
Lewis, O. "The Hyperventilation Syndrome." *British Journal of Psychiatry,* 1979, *135,* 367-368.
Linet, L. S. "Tourette Syndrome, Pimozide, and School Phobia: The Neuroleptic Separation Anxiety Syndrome." *American Journal of Psychiatry,* 1985, *142* (5), 613-615.
McDonald, J. E., and Sheperd, G. "School Phobia: An Overview." *Journal of School Psychology,* 1976, *14* (4), 291-305.
Marks, I. M. "Anxiety States Phobic and Obsessive-Compulsive Disorders. Clinical Picture, Differential Diagnostic and Management." *Progress in Neuropsychopharmacology,* 1981, *5* (2), 179-186.
Marks, I. "Are There Anticompulsive or Antiphobic Drugs? Review of the Evidence." *British Journal of Psychiatry,* 1983, *143,* 338-347.
Marks, I. M., and Gelder, M. "Different Ages of Onset in Varieties of Phobia." *American Journal of Psychiatry,* 1966, *123,* 218-221.
Marx, J. L. " 'Anxiety Peptide' Found in Brain." *Science,* 1984, *227,* 934.
Matson, J. L. "Exploration of Phobic Behavior in a Small Child." *Journal of Behavior Therapy and Experimental Psychiatry,* 1983, *14* (3), 257-259.
Michael, C. M., Morris, D. P., and Soroker, E. "Follow-up Studies of Shy, Withdrawn Children. II. Relative Incidence of Schizophrenia." *American Journal of Orthopsychiatry,* 1957, *27,* 331-337.

Mikkelsen, E. J., Detlor, J., and Cohen, D. J. "School Phobia Triggered by Haloperidol in Patients with Tourette's Disorder." *American Journal of Psychiatry,* 1981, *138* (12), 1572-1576.

Miller, L. C., Barrett, C. L., Hampe, E., and Noble, H. "Factor Structure of Childhood Fears." *Journal of Consulting and Clinical Psychology,* 1972, *39* (2), 264-268.

Nee, L. E., Caine, E. D., Polinsky, R. J., Eldridge, R., and Ebert, M. H. "Gilles de la Tourette Syndrome: Clinical and Family Study of 50 Cases." *Annals of Neurology,* 1980, 7 (1), 41-49.

Nesteros, J. N. "Gabaergic Mechanisms and Anxiety: An Overview and a New Neurophysiological Model." *Canadian Journal of Psychiatry,* 1984, *29,* 520-529.

Öst, L. G., and Hugdahl, K. "Acquisition of Phobias and Anxiety Response Patterns in Clinical Patients." *Behavior Research and Therapy,* 1981, *19,* 439-447.

Patterson, G. R. "An Empirical Approach to the Classification of Disturbed Children." *Journal of Clinical Psychology,* 1964, *20,* 326-337.

Paul, S. M., Marangos, P. J., Goodwin, F. N., and Skolnick, P. "Brain-Specific Benzodiazepine Receptors and Putative Endogenous Benzodiazepine-like Compounds." *Biological Psychiatry,* 1980, *15* (3), 407-428.

Pritchard, M., and Graham, P. "An Investigation of a Group of Patients Who Have Attended Both the Child and Adult Department of the Same Psychiatric Hospital." *British Journal of Psychiatry,* 1966, *112,* 603-612.

Rachman, S. "The Conditioning Theory of Fear Acquisition: A Critical Examination." *Behaviour Research and Therapy,* 1977, *15,* 375-387.

Rajecki, D. W., Lamb, M. E., and Obmascher, P. "Toward a General Theory of Infantile Attachment: A Comparative Review of Aspects of the Social Bond." *Behavioral and Brain Sciences,* 1978, *3,* 415-464.

Rapoport, J., Elkins, R., Langer, D. H., Sceery, W., Buschsbaum, M. S., Gillin, J. C., Murphy, D. L., Zahn, T. P., Lake, R., Ludlow, C., and Mendelson, W. "Childhood Obsessive-Compulsive Disorder." *American Journal of Psychiatry,* 1981, *138* (12), 1545-1554.

Rapoport, J., Elkins, R., and Mikkelsen, E. "Clinical Controlled Trial of Chlorimipramine in Adolescents With Obsessive-Compulsive Disorder." *Psychopharmacology Bulletin,* 1980, *16,* 61-63.

Robins, L. N. *Deviant Children Grown Up.* Baltimore: Williams and Wilkins, 1966. (Reprinted Huntington, N.Y.: Krieger, 1974.)

Robins, L. N. "Follow-up Studies." In H. C. Quay and J. S. Werry (eds.), *Psychopathological Disorders of Childhood,* New York: Wiley, 1979.

Rutter, M. L. "Relationships Between Child and Adult Psychiatric Disorders." *Acta Psychiatrica Scandinavica,* 1972, *48,* 3-21.

Rutter, M. "Attachment and the Development of Social Relationships." In M. Rutter (ed.), *Scientific Foundations of Developmental Psychiatry.* Baltimore: University Park Press, 1981a.

Rutter, M. "Emotional Development." In M. Rutter (ed.), *Scientific Foundations of Developmental Psychiatry,* Baltimore: University Park Press, 1981b.

Rutter, M., and Shaffer, D. "DSM-III: A Step Forward or Back in Terms of the Classification of Child Psychiatric Disorders?" *Journal of the American Academy of Child Psychiatry,* 1980, *19,* 371-394.

Rutter, M., Tizard, J., and Whitmore, K. *Education, Health, and Behavior: Psychological and Medical Study of Childhood Development.* London: Longman, 1970. (Reprinted Huntington, N.Y.: Krieger, 1981.)

Shapiro, A. K., Shapiro, E. S., Bruun, R. D., and Sweet, R. D. *Gilles de la Tourette Syndrome.* New York: Raven Press, 1978.

Sheehan, D. V., Sheehan, K. E., and Minichiello, W. E. "Age of Onset of Phobic Disorders: A Reevaluation." *Comprehensive Psychiatry,* 1981, *22* (6), 544-553.

Skolnick, P., Ninan, P., Insel, T., Crawley, J., and Paul, S. "A Novel Chemically Induced Animal Model of Human Anxiety." *Psychopathology,* 1984, *17* (suppl. 1), 25-36.

Stewart, M. A., and Gath, A. *Psychological Disorders of Children.* Baltimore: Williams and Wilkins, 1978.

Terr, L. C. "Chowchilla Revisited: The Effects of Psychic Trauma Four Years After a School-Bus Kidnapping." *American Journal of Psychiatry,* 1983, *140* (12), 1543-1550.

Torgersen, S. "Genetic Factors in Anxiety Disorders." *Archives of General Psychiatry,* 1983, *40,* 1085-1089.

Ultee, C. A., Griffioen, D., and Schellekens, J. "The Reduction of Anxiety in Children: A Comparison of the Effects of 'Systematic Desensitization in Vitro' and 'Systematic Desensitization in Vivo'," *Behaviour Research and Therapy,* 1982, *20,* 61-67.

Valzelli, L. "Gilles de la Tourette's Syndrome: An Overview." In W. V. Essman and L. Valzelli (eds.), *Neuropharmacology: Clinical Applications.* New York: Spectrum, 1982.

Van Winter, J. T., and Stickler, G. B. "Panic Attack Syndrome." *Journal of Pediatrics,* 1984, *105* (4), 661-665.

Warren, W. "Some Relationships Between the Psychiatry of Childen and of Adults." *Journal of Mental Science,* 1960, *106,* 815-826.

Werry, J. S., and Aman, M. G. "Anxiety in Children." In G. D. Burrows and B. M. Davies (eds.), *Handbook of Studies on Anxiety.* Amsterdam: ASP Biological and Medical Press, 1980.

Wolpe, J. "The Dichotomy Between Classical Conditioned and Cognitively Learned Anxiety." *Journal of Behavior Therapy and Experimental Psychiatry,* 1981, *12,* 35-42.

Yule, W., Sacks, B., and Hersov, L. "Successful Flooding Treatment of a Noise Phobia in an Eleven-Year-Old." *Journal of Behavior Therapy and Experimental Psychiatry,* 1974, *5,* 209-211.

James H. L. Beeghly is an assistant professor of psychiatry at the University of Iowa Hospitals and Clinics, Iowa City, Iowa.

Anxiety disorder clinics are sophisticated medical centers that require careful planning and dedicated execution by a team of specialized professionals.

The Anxiety Disorders Clinic

Susan Dourney Erskine

The goal of a specialty clinic is to allocate resources for a group of patients who suffer from the same or related psychiatric disorders. A psychiatric specialty clinic is similar to other types of medical clinics in that both evaluate the common and unusual presentations and management problems posed by a given disorder (Nasrallah, 1984).

There are many specialty psychiatric clinics in both the private and the public sectors, and more will open in the future. The number of specialty psychiatric clinics in multi-hospital systems, for example, rose from eighteen in 1983 to twenty-nine in 1984, a 62 percent increase. While inpatient admissions are expected to decrease 25 percent by 1990, outpatient services should increase proportionately (Wallace, 1985).

The trend in psychiatry, as in the health care field in general, is to develop cost-efficient systems of care, utilizing outpatient services whenever possible. Disorder-specific therapies, including biological and psychological interventions based on specific diagnosis, were cited as a major treatment issue for the next decade in a survey of psychiatric experts. A specialty clinic can serve as a center for assessment, treatment, and follow-up for patients with anxiety disorders (Strauss and others, 1984).

This chapter will discuss the development, organization, and services of an anxiety disorders clinic. Strategies for marketing the services of a clinic will also be reviewed.

R. A. Muñoz (ed.). *Treating Anxiety Disorders.*
New Directions for Mental Health Services, no. 32. San Francisco: Jossey-Bass, Winter 1986.

Development of an Anxiety Disorders Clinic

The development of a new health care service, such as an anxiety clinic, involves a series of planning stages designed to eliminate future problems. This process will be useful in identifying obstacles, determining the central direction of the project, and identifying specific issues to be dealt with in order to proceed smoothly (Rubright and MacDonald, 1981).

Understanding the Marketplace

The first stage in the development of a clinic is understanding the environment or marketplace where the clinic will be located: existing providers, consumers of the services to be rendered, and available support. Identifying existing providers involves looking at other institutions or individuals in the area that offer services or programs similar to those of the proposed clinic. For example, a psychiatrist or group of psychiatrists may be known for treating anxiety patients, or a local university may have an anxiety clinic. Often psychologists, counselors, or social workers may be treating phobias and anxiety disorders. One source for identifying existing providers in a geographic area is the National Phobia Treatment Directory (available from the Phobia Society of America, 5820 Hubbard Dr., Rockville, MD 20852). Once the providers have been identified, an evaluation can be made of the quality of the services they provide and how extensive their penetration of the marketplace has been.

Understanding may be gained by talking to people in the community who provide or use the services and know what the needs are. These people are called *key informants* and may include other mental health professionals, hospital administrators, social service agency personnel, employee assistance personnel in local industry, and academicians. Anxiety patients are good key informants because often they have utilized the services of many providers in the area.

Key informants permit establishing a position in the marketplace, some starting objectives, and the initial strategies for marketing. The survival of the clinic is based on attracting those who need its services. This does not always have a direct relationship to the extent of the need. In establishing this type of specialty clinic the goal is utilization of the services offered, not necessarily provision of additional services in an area.

Establishing Objectives

The next stage in planning the anxiety clinic involves establishing objectives. This process should be carried out as a team effort with the people who will be involved in the project. Information that was gained in the first stage of planning—understanding the environment—should now be utilized to increase the chance of the new services being accepted in the community (Cooper, 1979).

The preliminary objectives form the framework for the project. An example of a preliminary objective may be to become a formidable and respected resource for diagnosing and treating anxiety patients. Once the preliminary objectives are identified, *obstacles* and *opportunities* are detailed.

The obstacles need to be assessed realistically so that they can be dealt with. One might be gaining the support of physicians who are treating anxiety patients, including family practice, internal medicine, and OB/GYN specialists.

One study found that seventy percent of a group of anxiety patients had consulted more than ten physicians (Sheehan, 1983). As it is likely that many of the target consumers are currently part of the practice of another physician, the clinic may develop a system that insures that physicians are kept up to date on the progress of their patients and that the patients return to their primary physicians.

The opportunities can be thought of as the silver lining of the project. For example, the community in which the clinic is to be developed may have no comparable program, or a local hospital staff may be willing to sponsor a clinic. A list of opportunities helps to guide the project along favorable lines.

Once existing providers and target consumers of services have been looked at, peripheral support should be assessed. Support from the medical community can be encouraged by involving many physicians in the planning of the clinic. If their opinions are sought and incorporated into the development of the clinic, it is more likely that they will support the end product.

Financial support analysis needs to include an estimated budget and realistic assessment of reimbursement for services. Financial support must also be assessed from the standpoint of both beginning the clinic and ongoing reimbursement for services.

Choosing the Facility

Where to locate the anxiety clinic is the next variable to consider in the development process. Two locations will be discussed in this section: a free-standing clinic and a clinic located within the confines of an acute hospital, either general or psychiatric. An anxiety clinic may be one of several outpatient psychiatric clinics within a hospital or a single service, depending on resources and needs.

Hospital Clinic. The benefits to developing an anxiety clinic within an acute hospital include the following:

1. The ancillary services required in the evaluation and manage-

ment of the patient are readily available. These include laboratory, radiology, pharmacy, and social services.

2. In the eyes of the prospective patient, a clinic situated in a hospital often has more status than a free-standing clinic. The hospital somehow adds an image of stability. This perception may be changing among today's consumers as cost becomes a major factor in making choices and economical free-standing facilities proliferate.

3. The hospital can market the services of the clinic as part of its larger marketing plan.

4. The hospital can contract with various HMO's, PPO's, and health plans, with the services of the clinic included in the package.

5. Physicians on the medical staff of the hospital may become part of the referral network.

6. The clinic can enhance the inpatient psychiatric program by providing after-care services for patients discharged from the hospital.

Development of the clinic with the hospital can be achieved in three ways.

Hospital-Run Clinic. In this model the administration of the hospital decides to develop a clinic and hires a medical director and personnel to staff the clinic. The hospital absorbs all costs in running the clinic and collects the revenue generated by the clinic. Physicians working in the clinic are paid a fee for services or a straight salary. In the model the hospital establishes its identity as a provider of a mental health service to the community.

The hospital-run clinic depends heavily on direct consumer marketing services and community referral sources.

Physician-Hospital Joint Venture. A physician or group of physicians who have a special interest or expertise in diagnosing and treating anxiety disorders may contract with a hospital to develop an anxiety disorders clinic. There are various ways to structure the relationship according to the needs of the facilities and physicians. One way would be sharing revenues of the costs incurred by the hospital versus the costs incurred by the physicians in the areas of billing and collection, supplies, office space, personnel, and marketing. Another type of arrangement would be to have the physicians bill their services and the hospital provide the space needed to operate the clinic.

In a joint venture the hospital benefits through increased utilization of its ancillary services, increased referrals to the inpatient unit, and direct revenues generated by the clinic. The physicians benefit by increasing their patient population while developing their skills in diagnosing and treating anxiety patients. With a standardized approach to the collection of clinical information, opportunities for research become available.

Freestanding Clinic. A freestanding clinic may be developed either as part of an existing psychiatric practice or as a separate entity. The space required for a clinic is minimal. Office space for support personnel and records storage, a group room, and an office for consultation with the patient and the family are the minimum requirements. The group room should be large enough to comfortably seat ten to fifteen people; it may have a blackboard, a table, and bookshelves for displaying educational materials. The group room may double as a waiting room. If the chosen facility does not include a room large enough for a group, arrangements can often be made with local churches, schools, or libraries for a room large enough to conduct group activities.

Whether the anxiety clinic is to be located in a hospital, in a freestanding facility, or in an existing practice, it is important that it have a clear identity. The patient should be able to identify with that facility as the central location for his evaluation and treatment. Physicians and support staff should come to the facility to see the patient, so that patients are not shuffled to various locations.

Personnel

The anxiety disorders clinic is staffed by a multidisciplinary team under the direction of a psychiatrist or group of psychiatrists. Other models of staffing exist but this is the model that will be proposed in this section. The staffing patterns will need to be adapted to suit each clinic's needs and resources.

The psychiatrist acts as the team leader and coordinator of care for the individual patients. A disorder-specific clinic provides an opportunity for the psychiatrist to increase his or her skill in diagnosing and treating anxiety disorders because of the increased number of patients. Knowledge and skill, however, are not the psychiatrist's only attributes for treating anxiety patients. Sensitivity and the ability to deal with neurotic behavior are equally important (Clancy and others, 1983).

Anxiety patients are sometimes misunderstood by physicians and often become convinced that they have a serious physical condition. This often leads to a loss of confidence in the medical profession. Many patients develop maladaptive behavior, which is an attempt to cope with or prevent anxiety. The resulting preoccupation with health and the fear of physical illness restrict social and occupational activities. Since this situation must be considered the rule rather than the exception, the psychiatrist must be able to deal with it in order to anticipate problems in managing the case.

Other physicians should also be part of the treatment team on a consulting basis. The psychiatrist can work with an internist and/or cardiologist to develop a protocol for routine physical screening and lab work and to set criteria for referring patients when necessary. Patients may be referred either to their personal physician or to the internist who is working with the clinic.

Having an internist or cardiologist involved in the clinic is useful also from a marketing standpoint. Many anxiety patients are reluctant to view their problem as a psychiatric illness. They may be more accepting of seeking treatment knowing that the physical aspects of their illness are also being carefully evaluated.

Nonphysician members of the treatment team will vary according to the needs and location of the clinic. Personnel needs should be assessed from both a therapeutic and a financial standpoint. Because of the need to price services competitively, it is important to create a "cost efficient" staffing mix (Fenton and others, 1984).

In a small clinic a psychiatrist may provide the pharmacologic treatment as well as behavioral and family therapies. In a larger clinic a psychologist skilled in the techniques of in vivo exposure may provide the behavioral therapies and run groups. Social workers or marriage and family counselors may assist in working with the patient's family. New members of the team should have the sensitivity to work with the psychiatrist who is directing the treatment. From the financial standpoint, it is also important to consider third-party payer reimbursement for the services. Regulations of Medicaid, Champus, and other third-party payers must be reviewed with respect to covered services.

An administrator may be employed to coordinate all the nonmedical aspects of the clinic. The administrator would be responsible for marketing, patient flow, and billing and collection services. Depending on the size and location of the clinic, the administrator may also handle personnel, payroll, and accounting functions. Since the physicians and other treatment professionals may have only a portion of their time allocated to the clinic, the administrative person pulls it all together. The administrator should have a business background, knowledge of medical office management, and ability to market the clinic services in the community. The administrative position in a small clinic could be filled by a qualified nurse or social worker who could then also assist in the treatment process.

The key to staffing a successful anxiety clinic is to achieve a mix of professions who communicate and work well together, with knowledge, expertise, enthusiasm, flexibility, and sensitivity in treating anxiety patients. They should be able to utilize their skills in a cost-efficent manner.

Services Provided

Specific treatment modalities are discussed in other chapters of this book. This section will focus on the organizaton of services to provide a climate for the optimal effectiveness of these modalities.

Initial Assessment and Diagnosis

The first contact with the anxiety disorder patient must be handled carefully to create a favorable climate for long-term treatment. A supportive relationship is the first priority, as there is little hope that the patient will continue treatment without a good beginning (Clancy and Noyes, 1981).

A detailed history should be obtained by either the physician or a member of the treatment team. If a nonphysician is going to conduct the initial interview, the patient should be advised of the treatment-team approach used at the clinic and the value of this approach. Part of the initial assessment may include having the patient complete anxiety scales such as those suggested by Sheehan (1983) (see Figures 1 and 2). Scales can be useful in objectively documenting symptoms and judging improvement once treatment has begun. They help patients feel that the range and severity of symptoms are being carefully evaluated by the physican. The use of scales may not be appropriate for patients who are already sensitive to a range of symptoms and who might be alarmed by this new source of concern (Clancy and others, 1983).

The second step of the evaluation, as mentioned in the chapter on diagnosis, rules out a medical illness that may be causing the anxiety symptoms. The psychiatrist, in conjunction with the consulting medical specialists, should devise a protocol that would include a complete physical, with laboratory and diagnostic tests as indicated. The patient's previous medical records should be obtained and reviewed to avoid unnecessary duplication of tests. If a medical illness is diagnosed, treatment would be provided by the consulting medical specialist. The patient who is found to have medical illness may benefit by continued support and consultation with the anxiety clinic staff.

Once the diagnosis has been made, the psychiatrist will meet with other members of the treatment team to decide on the individual treatment plan. Next, the patient, and family when appropriate, learn about the diagnosis and expected treatment plan.

The patient's perceptions and expectations of drug therapy should be explored, and the psychiatrist should discuss both the benefits and the limitations of anti-anxiety medications. Patients benefit from medication education and the establishment of treatment goals with realistic expectations (Nasdahl and others, 1985).

Several services may be provided by the anxiety clinic to assist the patient in both the initial treatment and the long-term management. These services may be provided solely by the psychiatrist in a small clinic or with the assistance of other mental health professionals in a larger clinic.

Education. Education of the patient and the family is crucial in achieving treatment goals. Education about the nature of anxiety disorders may be done informally, through reading materials and discussion, or formally, in a group setting.

Understanding the nature of the problem will help patients and family feel more in control of the situation. Specific techniques for controlling anxiety and managing stress may be taught in a group setting.

Figure 1. Part 1: Patient-Rated Anxiety Scale

Instructions: Below is a list of problems and complaints that people sometimes have. Circle the number to the right that best describes how much that problem bothered or distressed you during the past six months. Mark only one number for each problem and do not skip any items.

0—Not at all 1—A little bit 2—Moderately 3—Markedly 4—Extremely

HOW MUCH WERE YOU BOTHERED BY:

1. Lightheadedness, faintness, or dizzy spells	0	1	2	3	4
2. Sensation of rubbery or "jelly" legs	0	1	2	3	4
3. Feeling off balance or unsteady as if about to fall	0	1	2	3	4
4. Difficulty in getting breath or overbreathing	0	1	2	3	4
5. Skipping or racing of the heart	0	1	2	3	4
6. Chest pain or pressure	0	1	2	3	4
7. Smothering or choking sensation or lump in throat	0	1	2	3	4
8. Tingling or numbness in parts of the body	0	1	2	3	4
9. Hot flashes or cold chills	0	1	2	3	4
10. Nausea or stomach problems	0	1	2	3	4
11. Episodes of diarrhea	0	1	2	3	4
12. Headaches or pains in neck or head	0	1	2	3	4
13. Feeling tired, weak, and exhausted easily	0	1	2	3	4
14. Spells of increased sensitivity to sound, light, or touch	0	1	2	3	4
15. Bouts of excessive sweating	0	1	2	3	4
16. Feeling that surroundings are strange, unreal, foggy or detached	0	1	2	3	4
17. Feeling outside or detached from part or all of your body or a floating feeling	0	1	2	3	4
18. Worrying about your health too much	0	1	2	3	4
19. Feeling you are losing control or going insane	0	1	2	3	4
20. Having a fear that you are dying or that something terrible is about to happen	0	1	2	3	4
21. Shaking or trembling	0	1	2	3	4
22. Unexpected waves of depression occurring with little or no provocation	0	1	2	3	4
23. Emotions and moods going up and down a lot in response to changes around you	0	1	2	3	4
24. Being dependent on others	0	1	2	3	4
25. Having to repeat the same action in a ritual (e.g., checking, washing, counting repeatedly, when it's not really necessary)	0	1	2	3	4
26. Recurrent words or thought that persistently intrude on your mind and are hard to get rid of (e.g., unwanted aggressive, sexual, or poor impulse-control thoughts)	0	1	2	3	4
27. Difficulty in falling asleep	0	1	2	3	4
28. Waking up in the middle of the night or restless sleep	0	1	2	3	4
29. Avoiding situations because they frighten you	0	1	2	3	4
30. Tension and inability to relax	0	1	2	3	4
31. Anxiety, nervousness, restlessness	0	1	2	3	4
32. Sudden unexpected panic spells that occur with little or no provocation (e.g., anxiety attacks with three or more of the symptoms listed above occurring together)	0	1	2	3	4

Figure 1. *(continued)*

33.	Sudden unexpected spells like those listed above, without full panic, that occur with little or no provocation (e.g., attacks associated with only one or two symptoms)	0	1	2	3	4
34.	Anxiety episodes that build up as you anticipate doing something and that are more intense than most people experience in such situations	0	1	2	3	4
35.	Surges of panic that occur while you are in the phobic situation	0	1	2	3	4

Source: Sheehan, 1983.

Figure 2. Part 2: Patient-Rated Anxiety Scale

Instructions: Circle one of the numbers to the right of each question to describe how you feel right now.

0—Not at all 1—A little bit 2—Moderately 3—Markedly 4—Extremely

1.	Mouth drier than usual	0	1	2	3	4
2.	Worried, preoccupied	0	1	2	3	4
3.	Nervous, jittery, anxious, restless	0	1	2	3	4
4.	Afraid, fearful	0	1	2	3	4
5.	Tense, "uptight"	0	1	2	3	4
6.	Shaky inside or out	0	1	2	3	4
7.	Fluttery stomach	0	1	2	3	4
8.	Warm all over	0	1	2	3	4
9.	Sweaty palms	0	1	2	3	4
10.	Rapid or heavy heartbeat	0	1	2	3	4
11.	Tremor of hands or legs	0	1	2	3	4

Scoring Key

Part 1

Score	6–30	mild endogenous anxiety
Score	31–50	moderate endogenous anxiety
Score	51–80	marked endogenous anxiety
Score	81–134	severe endogenous anxiety

Part 2

Score	4–11	mild exogenous anxiety or phobia
Score	12–22	moderate exogenous anxiety or phobia
Score	23–33	marked exogenous anxiety or phobia
Score	34–44	severe exogenous anxiety or phobia

Source: Sheehan, 1983.

Figure 3. Personal Record

Date: ____________

Skills Used:

1. Thought stopping
2. Ventilation
3. Progressive relaxation
4.
5.
6.

Directions: Whenever you feel anxious or have a panic attack, note the time, place, and description of the situation below. Describe any skills that you used to reduce your anxiety, then rate the effectiveness of the skill in reducing the anxiety.

Reduction of Anxiety

Time	*Place*	*Description of Situation*	*Skills Used*	*Degree of Success*			
				very successful 10	*successful* 7	*moderately successful* 5	*didn't work* 0
3 p.m.	school	worrying about upcoming quiz	1–3		×		
11 p.m.	home	trying to go to sleep	2–3			×	

Patients should then be encouraged to practice these techniques at home and keep a record of their progress. Such techniques include thought stopping, self-monitoring, progressive relaxation, and ventilation skills. Once the techniques are taught and practiced, patients can be encouraged to keep a personal record of their anxiety and its reduction. Figure 3 shows an example of a personal record. A personal record can be useful also in monitoring side effects from medications and the reduction in the number of symptoms with treatment.

Ancillary Services. Anxiety disorders clinics provide several services that enhance the potential for rehabilitation. These services are the result of a careful assessment of existing services and the needs of the patient population.

Group Therapy. Group therapy may be appropriate for some patients and may be conducted by a psychologist or licensed counselor under the supervision of the psychiatrist. Group therapy may be useful in providing encouragement and support in the initial stages of treatment. It can also be useful for specific behavioral therapies utilized in treating phobic patients.

Family Therapy. The impact of anxiety disorders is felt not only by the patient but also by the spouse and family. The family's role in treatment cannot be overemphasized. As the patient improves, a family's equilibrium can be disrupted. Families that have adjusted to the patient's dependent and restricted lifestyle may not be prepared for the sudden changes in activity patterns that improvement can bring (Lane, 1984).

A clinic may offer family support groups, as well as marriage and family counseling when appropriate. Family members may also be enlisted to provide the support necessary for the patient's re-exposure to phobic situations once the spontaneous panic and anxiety attacks are controlled through the use of medications (Sheehan, 1982).

Ongoing Support Groups. Social support for patients may be provided through the use of support groups. Support groups may belong to the clinic or to existing community agencies. Group facilitators can be recruited from the clinic's recovered patient population and trained by staff members. Support group members may develop personal contacts within the group, which may be helpful between sessions.

Marketing the Anxiety Clinic

Marketing the anxiety clinic is a process that begins in the initial stages of development. This section will define the process of marketing and suggest several strategies for marketing the anxiety clinic.

The Process of Marketing

Health care marketing is a fairly recent phenomenon that began in earnest in the late 1970's. Marketing, a term that is often misunderstood, is defined in as many ways as there are experts on the subject. Phillip Kotler, one of the first to apply marketing principles to the health care field, defines marketing as " the analysis, planning, implementation and control of carefully formulated programs designed to bring about voluntary exchanges of values with target markets for the purpose of achieving organizational objectives" (Kotler, 1976). Kotler's definition emphasizes that marketing is more than advertising, selling, or promoting; it is a system for carrying out carefully planned objectives.

The marketing process must begin in the early stages of the anxiety clinic development. There are five keys to successful marketing:

1. Understand the market;
2. Know your position in the market;
3. Establish objectives and strategies;
4. Develop a marketing plan or system;
5. Manage the marketing function.

The first two tasks are completed before the clinic even opens. They form the basis for developing the marketing plan. Methods for understanding the market and knowing your position in the market were discussed in the first section of this chapter. Where to go is the objective; how to get there is the strategy.

Four general marketing strategies will be discussed:

1. *Market Penetration:* increasing the appreciation of services in the area currently served;
2. *Market Development:* offering services to new markets;
3. *Product Development:* improving existing services;
4. *Diversification:* Providing a new service.

An anxiety disorders clinic can penetrate an existing market for psychiatric services. Most psychiatrists treat anxiety patients; in choosing to specialize, however, by setting up an anxiety clinic, the service of treating these patients increases in value. The value is awarded by the potential consumer, the patient. Specializing sets a group of psychiatrists apart from other providers of care. In marketing terms, creating a disorder specific clinic is product development or improving existing services.

The services of the anxiety clinic can also be offered to new markets. In the past the patient was the only purchaser of care. Today there are a number of purchasers, HMO's, PPO's, self-insured industries, insurance companies, and others who can provide new markets for the services of a clinic. The objectives and strategies form the basis for the marketing plan. A successful marketing plan takes into account the marketing mix, sometimes called the "Four P's"; product, promotion, place, and price. *Product* refers to the range of services to the consumer. *Promotion* is a form of communication to those who will use the product. The anxiety disorders clinic patient is likely to be a young adult, often female. In promotion, adverstising and public relations activities are helpful. *Place* refers to the delivery of the services being offered. *Price* is how much the service will cost the consumer, both financially and psychologically.

Place and price are often overshadowed by promotion in a marketing plan. Physicians reluctant to get involved in promoting a clinic can do much to market in the area of place and price. Specific strategies for developing a marketing plan for the anxiety clinic will be discussed in the next section.

The final key to a successful marketing process is to manage the marketing function. This can be done with the use of an outside agency or by an individual or team within the organization that guides and maintains the process.

In a small anxiety disorders clinic the administrator may take the responsibility for coordinating the marketing functions. Outside consultants may be used to develop advertising campaigns, promotional materials, and public relations.

In a joint venture clinic where a hospital is a partner, the marketing department of the hospital may handle the promotion of the clinic. The clinic staff and physicians should work closely with any outside agency hired to assist with marketing. It is best to seek out an agency with experience in the health care field.

Marketing a service such as psychiatric care is much different from marketing a tangible product such as detergent or hair spray. The potential user of the service must be provided with accurate information to be able to conceptualize the service and its benefits (Carman and Uhl, 1973).

Marketing Strategies for the Anxiety Clinic

The marketing process can be utilized to develop specific strategies that will target both the patient as consumer and physician who may refer to the clinic. Which strategies will be effective for a particular clinic will depend on factors of size, budget, and geographical location.

Advertising and promotional materials should be developed along the lines of normalizing psychiatric services: in other words, offering the services to potential patients in a way that does not interfere with their image of themselves as normal (White, 1985). A good marketing program will try to reduce the fear and misunderstanding that many people have about psychiatric care (Pinkert, 1985).

In addition, the materials developed should stress that the clinic provides a comprehensive medical approach to treatment of anxiety disorders. Patients are most likely to respond to this approach, because they may view exclusively psychiatric care as a rejection of the legitimacy of their physical complaints. The goal of any type of advertising is to get a potential consumer to use the service that is being offered. Figure 4 shows a pyramid that depicts the stages that a potential consumer must go through before deciding to take action.

The first step is to create an awareness of the services offered. It can be achieved in several ways.

Figure 4. Objectives of Advertising

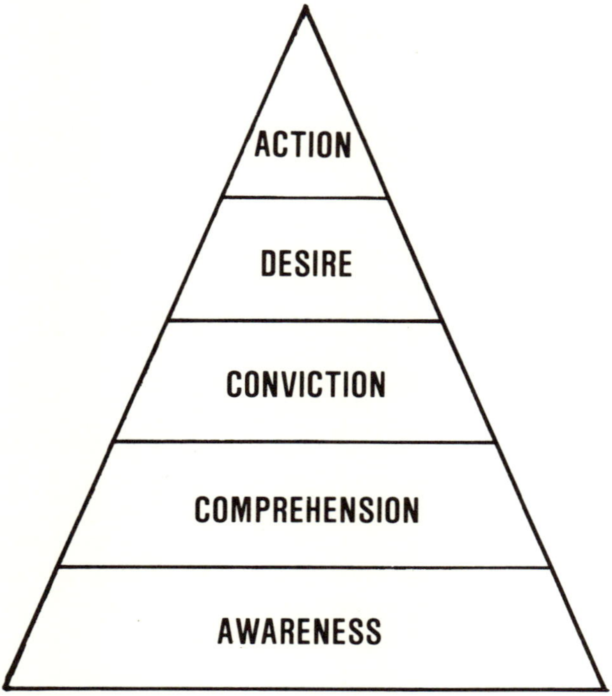

News Releases. News releases can be generated by an anxiety clinic when it opens and at various times throughout the year. Figure 5 shows a sample news release. Colorful paper, a striking letterhead, and personal contacts help to insure that a news release will be noticed among the hundreds that are mailed each day.

Public Service Announcements (PSA's). PSA's are new releases or audio or video tapes submitted for use on radio and TV stations. PSA's generally rely on an emotional appeal for action and differ from advertisements in that they must be educational or for a nonprofit activity. They can be used to announce free community lectures or screenings.

Community Education. Speakers from an anxiety clinic can give presentations to various community groups. Targeting specific goups that are more likely to utilize the services is an efficient way to schedule lectures.

Professional Education. Physicians, other mental health professionals, nurses, and social service agency personnel all may refer patients to an anxiety clinic. Often they meet in collegial groups on a monthly basis and look for speakers. Continuing education is another effective way of gaining exposure for an anxiety clinic. Staff development and medical staff coordinators in hospitals generally set up continuing education programs for the medical and nursing staff. An example of a continuing education

Figure 5. Sample Press Release

THE CENTER FOR ANXIETY DISORDERS
CONTACT: MARY SMITH 222-5151
HARBOR VIEW HOSPITAL
120 ELM STREET
SAN DIEGO, CA

FOR IMMEDIATE RELEASE

ANXIETY DISORDERS CLINIC OPENS
Anxiety disorders affect almost 5 percent of the population at a given time, producing a variety of symptoms ranging from choking sensations, difficult breathing, and heart palpitations to fears of losing control or of dying. The symptoms usually begin in the late teens or early twenties, and the disease strikes women three times as often as men.

The symptoms that characterize anxiety disorders were once thought to be entirely psychological in nature. Recent research indicates that there is a biological basis for the disease and that the disease appears to run in families.

The wide variety of symptoms suffered by anxiety disorders patients can mimic other illnesses, and victims often seek help from a multitude of medical specialties. This can lead to costly work-up, after which the patient may be told there is no organic basis for the problem. Anyone wishing more information about the Anxiety Disorders Clinic may call 555-1212.

---

seminar might be "Recognizing the Anxiety Disorder Patient" for emergency room staff at local hospitals.

Media Appearances. Local talk shows on radio and TV are a good medium for creating awareness of the services of an anxiety clinic.

Free Screenings. Utilizing PSA's and new releases, a clinic can advertise that they will do free anxiety screenings. The Sheehan scales (Figures 1 and 2) can be administered by a clinic staff member and easily scored. Treatment options can then be discussed with individuals who score high.

Information Hotlines. A clinic can advertise a phone number for free information about anxiety disorders. The person who handles these calls should appear knowledgeable and pleasant when talking to potential patients.

Phone Directory Listings. Phone directories present an opportunity to advertise the services of a clinic. White-page listings should appear in boldface print. Yellow-page listings should be placed under several headings such as "Mental health services," "Physicians," and "Clinics."

The phone company will generally work with the customer to develop a yellow-page advertisement that can be an effective tool in attracting potential patients. When setting up a clinic, it is important to check on the deadlines for yellow-page advertising in the particular location.

Collateral. Collateral comprises printed materials used in marketing a service. Printed materials can be used as a tool in the marketing program to help create an image of the clinic. A logo or a distinctive typeface for the name of the clinic should be carried through all printed materials, including brochures, letterheads, and business cards.

Brochures can be developed by an advertising firm or with the help of a graphic artist at a printing company. The latter option is less expensive but requires that the clinic staff be able to conceptualize and write the copy for the brochures. Brochures need to be developed with a target audience in mind. A brochure developed for patients may describe symptoms of anxiety disorders and emphasize the medical treatment provided. A brochure developed for potential referral sources such as other physicians may emphasize the fact that the referring physician will receive frequent reports on progress and that the patient will be returned at the completion of the treatment. Rolodex cards can be printed that describe the services of the clinic and how to refer a patient and that give the phone number and the address with a small map showing how to locate the clinic and where to park. Rolodex cards can be sent out with letters announcing the opening of the clinic to potential referral sources.

Several other patient-related marketing strategies should not be overlooked. These include

- A patient evaluation questionnaire to determine the patient's satisfaction with the service and environment
- Sending flowers to patients who are hospitalized
- Sending newsletters to patients to explain recent developments or discuss stress reduction and other educational topics
- Developing educational programs on video or audio tape
- Training clinic staff in guest relation techniques, including phone courtesy
- Offering a flexible schedule for patients who work
- Providing child care services in the clinic
- Developing a system for tracking clinic patients that includes name, referral source, type of insurance, age, sex, and other demographics that will help in understanding and maintaining the clinic's patient base.

The most important patient-related strategy concerns the physician-patient relationship. A recent Harris poll asked what people expect from their physicians. The majority said they wanted doctors to answer their questions openly and honestly, wanted problems explained in clear language, and wanted their doctor to spend enough time with them (Elsner, 1985). The best advertising campaign won't be of any use if the anxiety clinic physicians and staff don't provide a good service in the eyes of the patient.

Summary

This chapter proposes a framework for the development of an anxiety disorders clinic. This framework takes into account local resources and needs. Several alternatives are suggested for organization, staffing, and services. The marketing process and specific strategies for marketing are proposed not as a mandate but rather as an aid to be used in whatever way is appropriate under specific circumstances.

References

Carman, J. M., and Uhl, K. P. *Phillip and Duncan's Marketing Principles and Methods.* Homewood, Ill.: Irwin, 1973.

Clancy, J., and Noyes, R. "Anxiety Disorders: Management of Chronic Illness." *Journal of Clinical Psychiatry,* 1981, *42* (9), 330–333.

Clancy, J., Noyes, R., and Anderson, D. J. "Anxiety Behavior in Research Subjects." *Comprehensive Psychiatry,* 1983, *24* (6), 508–513.

Cooper, P. D. *Health Care Marketing,* Rockville, Md.: Aspen Systems, 1979.

Elsner, R. H. "Fewer Patients? Ask Yourself Why." *California Physician,* 1985, *2* (7), 13.

Fenton, W. S., Leaf, P. J., Moran, N. L., and Tischler, G. L. "Trends in Psychiatric Practice, 1965–1980." *American Journal of Psychiatry,* 1984, *141* (3), 346–351.

Kotler, P. *Marketing Management,* Englewood Cliffs, N.J.: Prentice-Hall, 1976.

Lane, L. "Panic Disorder Impact on the Family." *Diagnosis,* April 1984, 77–79.

Nasdahl, C. S., and others. "Protocols for the Use of Psychoactive Drugs. Part IV: Protocol for the Treatment of Anxiety Disorders." *Journal of Clinical Psychiatry,* 1985, *46,* 128–132.

Nasrallah, H. A. "The Clinic as a Teaching and Research Center." In R. A. Muñoz (ed.), *Potential for Mood Disorders Clinics.* New Directions for Mental Health Services, no. 23. San Francisco: Jossey-Bass, 1984.

Pinkert, M. S. *Hospital Survival Guide.* Rockville, Md.: Aspen Systems, 1985.

Rubright, R., and MacDonald, D. *Marketing Health and Human Services.* Rockville, Md.: Aspen Systems, 1981.

Sheehan, D. "Current Perspectives in the Treatment of Panic and Phobic Disorders." *Drug Therapy,* 1982, *12,* 179–190.

Sheehan, D. V. *The Anxiety Disease.* New York: Scribner's, 1983.

Strauss, G. D., Yager, J., and Strauss, G. E. "The Cutting Edge in Psychiatry." *American Journal of Psychiatry,* 1984, *141* (1), 38–43.

Wallace, C. "Ambulatory Care Facilities Multiply." *Modern Health Care,* 1985, *15* (12), 142–146.

White, E. "Centers Refine Their Advertising as Era of Soft-Peddling Ends." *Modern Health Care,* 1985, *15* (10), 74–75.

Susan Dourney Erskine is program administrator at the Western Mood and Sleep Disorders Institute and vice president of the Western Institute Foundation for Mental Health.

Somatic therapies have enhanced and improved the treatment of anxiety disorders. Their use requires attention of a number of factors discussed in this chapter.

Drug Therapy for Anxiety

Rodrigo A. Muñoz

Sheehan (1983) has proposed the following classification of medication useful in the treatment of patients suffering an anxiety disorder.

Monoamino Oxidase Inhibitors (MAO Inhibitors). Three are commonly used:

1. Phenelzine (Nardil)
2. Isocarboxazid (Marplan)
3. Tranylcypromine (Parnate)

Tricyclic Antidepressants (TCAs). There are many members of this class. The most widely used and studied are:

1. Imipramine (Tofranil)
2. Desipramine (Norpramin)
3. Amitriptyline (Elavil)
4. Nortriptyline (Pamelor)
5. Trimipramine (Surmontil)
6. Protriptyline (Vivactil)

Triazolopyridine

1. Trazodone (Desyrel)

Triazolobenzodiazepine

1. Alprazolam (Xanax)

As pointed out by Crammer and others (1978), the uses of monoamino oxidase inhibitors in psychiatry do not fall into neat categories.

R. A. Muñoz (ed.). *Treating Anxiety Disorders.*
New Directions for Mental Health Services, no. 32. San Francisco: Jossey-Bass, Winter 1986.

They may be considered as sedatives, euphoriants, antidepressants, and antiphobics. It is more rational, however, to think of them simply as having some slow modifying action on the central nervous system, changing the balance of brain functions in some as yet unknown way. "Some patients are undoubtedly helped by MAOI's, some even specifically by only one particular drug of the group" (Crammer and others, 1978). Phenelzine has been described as a drug with excellent effects on panic attacks, anticipatory anxiety, and phobias. It produces sedation, constipation, and hypotension but has limited anticholinergic effects. Starting with 45 mg daily, the dose may be gradually increased to 90 mg daily. Phenelzine should be given for six to eight weeks before the treatment is considered to have failed.

Imipramine and amitriptyline are the two oldest and best known tricyclic antidepressants. A recent survey of the members of the American Academy of Clinical Psychiatrists showed that these continue to be the antidepressants of choice for many practicing psychiatrists. Their use in panic attacks, anticipatory anxiety, and phobias is based on empirical consideration. Therapeutic effects are often obtained at doses of 150 mg or higher. TCAs may produce sedation, constipation, hypotension, and anticholinergic effects. They do not have the dietary restrictions that have been a problem in the use of monoamine oxidase inhibitors.

Trazodone is chemically unrelated to the tricyclic antidepressants. It does appear to be as effective, but it does not have the same anticholinergic effects and has a limited likelihood of cardiotoxicity. The initial dose is 150 mg a day in divided doses, which can be increased by 50 mg a day every three to four days. The average therapeutic dosage for outpatients is from 150 to 400 mg daily. Severely ill patients have been treated with 600 mg a day. Some clinicians give most of the daily dosage in the evening to take advantage of the sedative effect (*Medical Newsletter,* 1982). Prolonged painful erection of the penis has been reported with trazodone treatment in at least nine patients between twenty-four and sixty years old. Its use as a first-line drug of treatment in men should probably be limited to patients with prostatic enlargement or others for whom the absence of anticholinergic effects is a major advantage (*Medical Newsletter,* 1984).

Alprazolam is a benzodiazepine that is rapidly absorbed from the gastrointestinal tract, with peak blood levels in one to two hours. Most of the drug is metabolized, but an active metabolite is formed. The elimination half-life is about fourteen hours, which is comparable to the shorter-acting benzodiazepines such as lorazepam and oxazepam. In three large four-week double-blind trials, alprazolam was at least as effective as diazepam in treating outpatients with anxiety; alprazolam produced less drowsiness (*Medical Newsletter,* 1982). Most psychiatrists start alprazolam at .25 to .5 mg three times a day, which may be increased up to a maximum of 6 mg a day. In comparison to the tricyclics and the monoamino oxidase inhibitors, alprazolam is preferred by many because of absence of anticholinergic effects and much more rapid onset of action.

Special Issues in Drug Therapy

Anxiety and Depression. Breier and others (1985) have stressed that the concomitant occurrence of symptoms of generalized anxiety, panic attacks, and episodes of major affective disorders is well documented. The course of these disorders indicates a particularly strong relationship between panic and depression. Dealy and others (1981) divided a group of patients with anxiety neurosis into those who had a history of major depression and those who did not. Significantly more of the patients with major depression had a history of panic attacks. Patients with mixed symptoms seem to respond to a benzodiazepine (alprazolam), to tricyclic antidepressants, or to monoamino oxidase inhibitors. Future research will permit a comparison of the temporal efficacy and biochemical effect of antidepressant and antianxiety drugs in patients with panic disorder only, major depression only, and panic disorder with major depression.

Studying the psychiatric history of anxious patients, Breier and others (1984) reported on sixty subjects who were consecutively admitted to a sixteen-week outpatient clinic research treatment program for agoraphobia and panic disorders. Forty-one patients (68 percent) had a past or current episode of major depression, and thirty-five (85 percent) had endogenous-type major depression. Twenty patients (33 percent) had had an episode of primary major depression, and an average of three years separated the end of primary major depression and the first panic attack. Secondary major depression occurred in twenty-eight patients. This investigation demonstrated that major depression occurs in two-thirds of patients who come to an anxiety disorders clinic with agoraphobia or panic disorder; 50 percent of these patients have at least one major depressive episode prior to and, in most cases, temporarily separated from the onset of panic attacks. Patients with agoraphobia or panic disorder who have a history of major depression have a more severe anxiety disorder at the time of admission, greater levels of past impairment, and a longer duration of panic disorder as compared with patients with agoraphobia or panic disorder who have no history of depression.

Diagnostic studies and therapeutic trials may lend support to the suggestion that a distinct "anxious-depression" syndrome exists and should be recognized in a revision of DSM-III. By doing so, we may retrieve better data and depressed patients without anxiety may be treated in a different way (Lechman and others, 1983).

The Elderly. Age does not produce any consistent alterations in absorption of benzodiazepines (Thompson and others, 1983). As their pharmacokinetics may not change with age, the dosage of shorter-half-life benzodiazepines, such as alprazolam, may be similar to that in younger patients. A more serious concern with both benzodiazepines and other psychotropics is drug interaction, which requires a careful evaluation of other treatments the patient may be receiving.

If tricyclic antidepressants are to be used, the secondary amines (nortriptyline and desipramine) have been recommended. Older patients may have had prior episodes of depression. If they responded favorably to a specific medication, it should be used again. Treatment with tricyclics should last at least four weeks at a dosage adequate to produce either therapeutic effects or persistent side effects.

Monoamino oxidase inhibitors have also been used successfully in the elderly, especially in those with "atypical" depressions.

Finally, methylphenidate has been effective in older persons, especially those suffering medical problems (Katon and Raskind, 1980).

Abuse, Addiction, and Dependence. The concern here is with benzodiazepines. As aptly presented by Greenblatt and others (1983), "sensationalistic and terrifying depictions of benzodiazepine abuse and addiction have been a popular and recurrent subject of reporting in the lay media." In the late 1970s there were reports asserting the existence of a national epidemic of tranquilizer addiction attributable to a pharmaceutical industry that encouraged drug use and to a medical profession that overprescribed tranquilizers. That the concerns may have been exaggerated can be demonstrated by much evidence, including the actual drug use by major therapeutic classes (Baum and others, 1984). In 1981, medical compounds were ranked according to number of prescriptions written by physicians. Anti-infectives administered for systemic disorders were ranked first, followed by cardiovascular drugs. In 1981, prescriptions for diazepam, the only benzodiazepine among the top twenty-five drug chemicals, ranked sixth, far below hydrochlorothiazide, codeine, contraceptives, erythromycin, and propranolol.

Hollister and others (1981) and Rickels and others (1983) studied the effects of long-term use of diazepam. Hollister's patients took diazepam for periods of one month to sixteen years. Even with such a long-term use, diazepam seemed to retain its efficacy and did not lead to any clear-cut abuse. Rickels found that withdrawal was more likely after using the drug for more than eight months, was neither life-threatening nor incapacitating, and did not include convulsions or psychotic reactions. The withdrawal could be readily managed by gradually tapering the dose of the benzodiazepine. As mentioned by Rickels, two national U.S. household surveys conducted in 1971 and 1979 reported that anxiolytics were actually used rather infrequently and for short periods of time. Nevertheless, the 1979 survey found that 1.6 percent of subjects surveyed reported taking anxiolytic medication daily for one year or more, so a substantial subgroup of chronically anxious patients use benzodiazepines for prolonged periods of time.

Fears About MAOI's. A frequent comment in the psychiatric literature is that monoamino oxidase inhibitors are underused in the U.S., even though their effectiveness in agoraphobic-claustrophobic syndromes, social phobias, and panic attacks is well documented. The fears relate often to interaction with foods.

Pare (1985) has commented on how exaggerated the claims for interaction have been and how reports of adverse reactions have frequently been based on tenuous evidence. Over a ten-year period only seventeen cases of reactions known fatal between phenelzine and food stuffs had been reported in England at a time when phenelzine was one of the best-selling medications and also when "cheese reactions" were most likely to be reported.

There are many restrictions that no longer hold. As pointed out by Zisook (1985), adherence may be maximized by explaining the rationale for the restrictions and minimizing their number. As most food-related reactions have occurred because of the ingestion of aged or mature cheeses, they require the most attention. To the contrary, cottage, cream, and ricotta cheeses are permitted. Pickled, fermented, smoked, aged, and decaying meat, chicken, or fish should be avoided. Dairy products should be consumed fresh. Patients should drink clear spirits or white wine and avoid heavy beers, red wines, sherry or after dinner liquors.

Medications that contain sympathomimetic agents produce the most important drug interactions, requiring a clear warning to the patient and a discussion of any medications the patient may be taking. One may go a long way toward controlling reactions if the patient is warned not to start any prescribed or over-the-counter medication without consulting the therapist.

Side Effects of Antidepressants. Increasingly sophisticated patients consult about their medications and not infrequently have access to the PDR or other sources of information regarding possible side effects of prescription medications. Given the imposing list of possible side effects of tricyclics, the therapist should be aware that the manifestations reported by the patient may be produced by his or her depression and not by the prescription.

Nelson and others (1984) studied forty-three depressed inpatients during a three-week trial with desipramin hydrochloride. He used multiple regression analysis to examine the independent relationship of pretreatment symptoms, concurrent depression, and plasma drug concentration to subjective complaints reported during treatment. Subjective complaints were positively associated with pretreatment symptoms and the concurrent level of depression but not with plasma desipramine concentrations. Only two complaints, tremors and lightheadedness, were significantly associated with plasma drug concentration. The data indicated that during initial treatment of severe depression with desipramine, subjective complaints are most likely to be symptoms of depression and not side effects of the drug and that plasma desipramine determinations would not be useful for predicting or avoiding these complaints. The best strategy for dealing with the complaints was effective treatment for depression.

A new and most intriguing development in the study of response to tricyclic antidepressants is the investigation of that subgroup of patients who have a "true" therapeutic response. Quitkin and others (1984b) reported on 185 patients who participated in a six-week placebo-controlled drug trial. Substantially more patients receiving active than placebo medication displayed treatment-response patterns characterized by both two-week or greater delay in onset of initial improvement and nonfluctuating persistence of improvement once achieved. New studies of response patterns may permit better separation of placebo effect from true drug response.

Duration of Treatment. Before a treatment is abandoned, several factors have to be carefully evaluated. They include the patient's initial picture, his compliance, the possible side effects of medication, any concomitant medical disorders, and any other medications the patient may be taking. The pattern of change in symptoms may help in evaluating a partial response. Quitkin and others (1984a) have proposed that four factors are critical in determining the proportion of patients who respond favorably to antidepressant medication: diagnosis, type of drug, dose of drug, and duration of drug treatment. Their review of three placebo-controlled, randomized, antidepressant trials permitted the comparison of global clinical ratings at weekly intervals for patients receiving drugs and patients receiving placebo. They calculated the proportion of patients whose clinical status changed over time. A significant proportion of patients who showed no clear-cut response at four weeks showed much improvement at six weeks in drug but not placebo conditions.

The search for specific patterns of drug response in anxiety patients will be one of the exciting research fields in the years to come.

Propranolol and Stage Fright. Beta-blockers control several of the physiological manifestations of anxiety. If they are ingested before a performance that is usually accompanied by anxiety, the results may be spectacular. Goodwin (1986), in his excellent study on anxiety, describes experiments conducted with musicians who performed under the influence of a beta-blocker, propranolol. There was significant control of their fear, and their performance was enhanced. Many psychiatrists are using propranolol as the treatment of choice for symptoms that appear in specific anxiety-producing situations.

Conclusion

Much has been learned about the drug therapy of conditions associated with anxiety. Progress is expected in diagnosis, classification, and specific use of different treatments. In the meantime, the clinician today has at hand many useful ways of helping his patients.

References

Baum, C., Kennedy, D. L., Forbes, M. B., and others. "Drug Use in the United States in 1981." *Journal of the American Medical Association,* 1984, *251,* 1293-1297.

Breier, A., Charney, D. S., and Henninger, G. R. "The Diagnostic Validity of Anxiety Disorders and Their Relationship to Depressive Illness." *American Journal of Psychiatry,* 1985, *142,* 787-797.

Breier, A., Charney, D. S., and Henninger, G. R. "Major Depression in Patients with Agoraphobia and Panic Disorder." *Archives of General Psychiatry,* 1984, *41,* 1129-1135.

Crammer, Barraclough, and Heine. *The Use of Drugs in Psychiatry.* London: Gaskell, 1978.

Dealy, R. S., Ishiki, D. M., Avery, D. H., and others. "Secondary Depression in Anxiety Disorders." *Comprehensive Psychiatry,* 1981, *22,* 612-618.

Goodwin, D. W. *Anxiety.* New York: Oxford University Press, 1986.

Greenblatt, D. J., Shader, R. I., and Abernethy, D. R. "Current Status of Benzodiazepines." *The New England Journal of Medicine,* 1983, *309,* 410-416.

Hollister, L. E., Conley, F. K., Britt, R. H., and others. "Long Term Use of Diazepam." *Journal of the American Medical Association,* 1981, *246,* 1568-1570.

Katon, W., and Raskind, M. "Treatment of Depression in the Medically Ill Elderly with Methylphenidate." *American Journal of Psychiatry,* 1980, *137,* 3963-3965.

Lechman, J. F., Merikangas, K. R., Pauls, D. L., and others. "Anxiety Disorders and Depression: Contradictions Between Families Studied and the DSM-III Conventions." *American Journal of Psychiatry,* 1983, *140,* 880-886.

Medical Newsletter. New Rochelle, N.Y.: The Medical Letter, Inc., 1982, *24.*

Medical Newsletter. New Rochelle, N.Y.: The Medical Letter, Inc., 1984, *26.*

Nelson, J. C., Jatlow, P. I., and Quinlan, D. M. "Subjective Complaints During Desipramine Treatment." *Archives of General Psychiatry,* 1984, *41,* 55-59.

Pare, C.M.B. "The Present Status of Monoamino Oxidase Inhibitors." *British Journal of Psychiatry,* 1985, *146,* 576-584.

Quitkin, F. M., Rabkin, J. G., Russ, D., and others. "Duration of Antidepressant Drug Treatment." *Archives of General Psychiatry,* 1984a, *41,* 238-245.

Quitkin, F. M., Rabkin, J. G., Russ, D., and others. "Identification of True Drug Response to Antidepressants." *Archives of General Psychiatry,* 1984b, *41,* 782-786.

Rickels, K., Case, W. G., Downing, R. W., and others. "Long Term Diazepam Therapy and Clinical Outcome." *Journal of the American Medical Assocation,* 1983, *250,* 767-771.

Sheehan, D. V. *The Anxiety Disease.* New York: Scribner's, 1983.

Thompson, T. L., Moran, M. G., and Nies, A. S. "Psychotropic Drug Use in the Elderly." *The New England Journal of Medicine,* 1983, *308,* 134-138.

Zisook, S. "A Clinical Overview of Monoamino Oxidase Inhibitors." *Psychosomatics,* 1985, *26,* 240-246.

Rodrigo A. Muñoz is associate professor of clinical psychiatry at the University of California at San Diego, president of the American Academy of Clinical Psychiatrists, and president of the Western Mood and Sleep Disorders Institute in San Diego.

Index

D

E

N

O

P

Q

R

S

T

U.S. Postal Service

STATEMENT OF OWNERSHIP, MANAGEMENT AND CIRCULATION

Required by 39 U.S.C. 3685)

1A. TITLE OF PUBLICATION	1B. PUBLICATION NO.	2. DATE OF FILING
New Directions for Mental Health Services	4 9 3 9 1 0	9/26/86

3. FREQUENCY OF ISSUE	3A. NO. OF ISSUES PUBLISHED ANNUALLY	3B. ANNUAL SUBSCRIPTION PRICE
Quarterly	4	$30 indv/$40 inst

4. COMPLETE MAILING ADDRESS OF KNOWN OFFICE OF PUBLICATION *(Street, City, County, State and ZIP+4 Code) (Not printers)*

433 California St., San Francisco (SF County), CA 94104

5. COMPLETE MAILING ADDRESS OF THE HEADQUARTERS OF GENERAL BUSINESS OFFICES OF THE PUBLISHER *(Not printer)*

433 California St., San Francisco (SF County), CA 94104

6. FULL NAMES AND COMPLETE MAILING ADDRESS OF PUBLISHER, EDITOR, AND MANAGING EDITOR *(This item MUST NOT be blank)*

PUBLISHER *(Name and Complete Mailing Address)*

Jossey-Bass Inc., Publishers, 433 California St., S.F., CA 94104

EDITOR *(Name and Complete Mailing Address)*

H. Richard Lamb, Dept. of Psychiatry & Behavioral Sciences, USC School of Medicine, 1934 Hospital Place, Los Angeles, CA 90033

MANAGING EDITOR *(Name and Complete Mailing Address)*

William Henry, Jossey-Bass Publishers, 433 California St., S.F., CA 94104

7. OWNER *(If owned by a corporation, its name and address must be stated and also immediately thereunder the names and addresses of stockholders owning or holding 1 percent or more of total amount of stock. If not owned by a corporation, the names and addresses of the individual owners must be given. If owned by a partnership or other unincorporated firm, its name and address, as well as that of each individual must be given. If the publication is published by a nonprofit organization, its name and address must be stated.) (Item must be completed.)*

FULL NAME	COMPLETE MAILING ADDRESS
Jossey-Bass Inc., Publishers	433 California St., S.F., CA 94104

For names and addresses of stockholders, see attached list.

8. KNOWN BONDHOLDERS, MORTGAGEES, AND OTHER SECURITY HOLDERS OWNING OR HOLDING 1 PERCENT OR MORE OF TOTAL AMOUNT OF BONDS, MORTGAGES OR OTHER SECURITIES *(If there are none, so state)*

FULL NAME	COMPLETE MAILING ADDRESS
Same as #7	

9. FOR COMPLETION BY NONPROFIT ORGANIZATIONS AUTHORIZED TO MAIL AT SPECIAL RATES *(Section 423.12 DMM only)*
The purpose, function, and nonprofit status of this organization and the exempt status for Federal income tax purposes *(Check one)*

☐ (1) HAS NOT CHANGED DURING PRECEDING 12 MONTHS

☐ (2) HAS CHANGED DURING PRECEDING 12 MONTHS

(If changed, publisher must submit explanation of change with this statement.)

10. EXTENT AND NATURE OF CIRCULATION *(See instructions on reverse side)*	AVERAGE NO. COPIES EACH ISSUE DURING PRECEDING 12 MONTHS	ACTUAL NO. COPIES OF SINGLE ISSUE PUBLISHED NEAREST TO FILING DATE
A. TOTAL NO. COPIES *(Net Press Run)*	2000	2026
B. PAID AND/OR REQUESTED CIRCULATION 1. Sales through dealers and carriers, street vendors and counter sales	930	860
2. Mail Subscription *(Paid and/or requested)*	467	412
C. TOTAL PAID AND/OR REQUESTED CIRCULATION *(Sum of 10B1 and 10B2)*	1397	1272
D. FREE DISTRIBUTION BY MAIL, CARRIER OR OTHER MEANS SAMPLES, COMPLIMENTARY, AND OTHER FREE COPIES	88	203
E. TOTAL DISTRIBUTION *(Sum of C and D)*	1485	1475
F. COPIES NOT DISTRIBUTED 1. Office use, left over, unaccounted, spoiled after printing	515	551
2. Return from News Agents		
G. TOTAL *(Sum of E, F1 and 2 - should equal net press run shown in A)*	2000	2026

11. I certify that the statements made by me above are correct and complete

SIGNATURE AND TITLE OF EDITOR, PUBLISHER, BUSINESS MANAGER, OR OWNER

[signature] Vice President

PS Form 3526, Dec. 1985 *(See instruction on reverse)*